SOLVING
YOUR
SCRIPT

SOLVING
YOUR
SCRIPT

Tools and Techniques
for the Playwright

Jeffrey Sweet

HEINEMANN
PORTSMOUTH, NH

Heinemann
A division of Reed Elsevier Inc.
361 Hanover Street
Portsmouth, NH 03801–3912
www.heinemanndrama.com

Offices and agents throughout the world

Library of Congress Cataloging-in-Publication Data
Sweet, Jeffrey, 1950–
Solving your script : tools and techniques for the playwright / Jeffrey Sweet.
p. cm.
ISBN 0-325-00053-0 (pbk.: alk. paper)
1. Drama—Technique. 2. Playwriting. I. Title.

PN1661 .S85 2001
808.2—dc21

00-069958

Editor: Lisa A. Barnett
Production: Vicki Kasabian
Cover design: Darci Mehall/Aureo Design
Manufacturing: Steve Bernier

Printed in the United States of America on acid-free paper
05 04 03 02 01   DA   1 2 3 4 5

For Sheldon Harnick

CONTENTS

Contents

ACKNOWLEDGMENTS

My thanks to Lisa Barnett (my editor), Michele LaRue (who keeps an eye on me at *Back Stage*), and Mark Dahlby (who dragged me online).

INTRODUCTION

IN THE DRAMATIST'S TOOLKIT, I ARTICULATED THEORIES ON HOW TO approach various technical problems that arise when writing for stage and screen.

Since then, I have received a good deal of feedback, much of it gratifying. But some correspondents said that they wished I had included assignments in *Toolkit*. Surely, they wrote, if I had such concrete theories of dramatic writing, I must also have some ideas for challenges that might help writers develop skills. After all, knowledge that lifting weights will build muscles doesn't in itself build muscles. One actually has to lift the weights. And I'm here to show you how.

As it happens, I do a fair amount of teaching and I do indeed make assignments. During the course of several years of running workshops and classes, I've come up with a number that seem to be useful in helping students translate the abstraction of theory into practice. In the wake of the *Toolkit*'s publication, Lisa Barnett, my editor at Heinemann, raised the possibility of my putting together a book focusing on these.

I was still mulling what form this book should take when I received an e-mail from Mark Dahlby. He was organizing something called Writers on the Net, which offered writing courses via the Internet. Might I be interested in trying my hand at teaching in this manner? I was skeptical. Till then, all of my teaching had been hands-on and face-to-face, and I doubted how effective I could be without eye contact.

Mark prevailed upon me to give it a try for eight weeks. He assembled a group of students and put them and me on something called a listserv—a joint mailing list for e-mail—so that whatever I mailed to the listserv's address would be received by all of the students. Similarly, anything a student posted to the listserv would arrive to these same subscribers. And so I began to improvise my way through the first course.

I started by sending short lessons, the written equivalent of lectures. At the end of each, I would make an assignment designed to help the students put into practice the techniques I'd described. As each student posted a scene in response to the assignment, a copy of that scene went to everyone in the group. I would discuss their responses, again sending my comments to everyone on the list.

No, there was no eye contact, but the ability to comment with such detail and specificity offered its own opportunities. I continued to offer the course, refining it as I went along.

It occurred to me that these lessons, assignments, responses, and discussions might serve as the basis of a text that would convey some of the experience of being in a workshop, hence the structure of this book. I also illustrate these principles with excerpts from my plays. Yes, I know it's immodest, but to write a book like this is inherently immodest. Besides, the passages I quote are the product of my consciously employing the techniques I introduce, so you can judge for yourself whether what I recommend actually works. I quote a little from a couple of my early plays, *Responsible Parties* and *The Value of Names*, but most of the material I include is from *Bluff*, *Flyovers*, *I Sent a Letter to My Love*, and *With and Without*, plays I was writing during the years I was assembling material for this book. (Incidentally, the use of ". . . . ." in excerpts from my own work indicates that I'm skipping some material at that point in the original text.)

In addition, there are chapters I call Sidebars, essays on other aspects of dramatic writing that don't include corresponding assignments. Some of these began as articles for a "Playwright's Corner" column I wrote for *Back Stage*, though the material has undergone substantial revision.

As for the scenes from students and colleagues I reprint and on which I comment: I have chosen one or two of these for each lesson. Some are from my online classes, others are from my face-to-face classes, and a few are from friends I've dragooned into helping me. I want to thank all concerned for allowing me to reprint their work, especially given the fact that inevitably some of my comments concern those aspects I think could benefit from revision. But the scenes would have been less than useful for this book if they were all polished gems.

Please approach these pieces understanding that, though I hope they will entertain, they were not written to be complete and satisfying works unto themselves. They were composed by people trying to assimilate technique, and they are to finished pieces what Czerny piano exercises are to sonatas; their purpose is to stretch muscles, not to enrich the literature of the theatre. You will also probably notice a disproportionate percentage of these pieces focus on younger people, a reflection of the demographics of many of my classes. I suggest you read the scenes through first, then go back and reread them, referring to my notes.

Also, yes, I am aware that the tone of my comments in this book is doctrinaire. This is not meant to suggest that my opinion on these matters is the ultimate one, or that there is only one approach to any given scenic problem. (For instance, though I urge students to try writing mostly in the present or future tenses, I am well aware that there are occasions when writing in the past tense is effective.) Rather, I'm trying to make certain technical concepts vivid. I also repeat myself a little, to reinforce in response to different scenes what I view as the key concepts. This, too, is intended to mirror what would go on in a class.

The assignments included in this book address techniques for writing dramatic material for any dramatic medium, live or recorded. Though there are significant differences between writing for stage, TV, film, and radio (which I discuss in some detail in *The Dramatist's Toolkit*), I believe there are more similarities. In each of these arenas, the task is to write material actors will be able to play, and many of the craft ideas—such as negotiating over objects, exploring the characters' various voices and roles, using high-context exposition—apply alike to playscript, teleplay, radio script, and screenplay.

Inevitably there is some overlap of material with *The Dramatist's Toolkit*. In contrast to that book, which was primarily concerned with the articulation of theory, this one touches on theory in conjunction with a series of tasks designed to add tools to your reservoir of conscious technique. Inevitably, too, as some years have passed since I wrote *Toolkit*, what follows reflects new ideas or further permutations of ones I articulated in that book.

A word on the title, *Solving Your Script*. These lessons are presented in the hope that they will suggest ways of looking at and dealing with problems you encounter in your work. I offer these techniques with some confidence because I find them useful in my own writing, particularly when facing deadlines. I have been especially conscious of using these strategies when working for television, sometimes rewriting material that would be shot the next day or, in the capacity of a story editor, when working with a writer to polish a script.

For example, one writer I was working with was assigned to write an episode involving a woman who is held hostage for a year at a beach house by a strange but not insensitive man acting under the orders of an unseen villain. (How did you guess this was a soap opera?) Among the problems we encountered was how to convey the passage of time and how to suggest that the captor had other dimensions beyond the menacing.

Turning to the idea of negotiating over objects (introduced here in Lesson 2), I suggested that the captor pass his time carving sculptures out of the driftwood he finds on the beach. The sculptures implied an artistic or sensitive side. The driftwood reinforced the fact that the characters were living near the shore. And, as each new scene began by showing the presence of more of these sculptures in the house, the audience got the sense that time was passing. There was an additional benefit to giving the actor a scene in which he worked on a piece of wood with his knife: the knife registered both as a tool for making art (showing his sensitive side) and as a potentially deadly weapon (showing his threatening side).

Am I going to claim that this brought the episode up to the level of Chekhov? Nah. But it sharpened and heightened the material, and the actors had a lot more fun than they would have if they had done nothing in the scenes but talk at each other endlessly (pretty common in soap writing). And the head writers charting the show's plot were sufficiently taken with these additions that they returned to the character and made the destruction of his sculptures an important part of a later episode.

I do not pretend or hope that this book is as orderly a presentation as *Toolkit* was. Sometimes a student's response to an assignment leads to exploring tangential issues. This, too, is intended to reflect the nature of a real class—yes, one tries to concentrate on the "official" topic of the moment, but there's no point in being so rigid as to bypass the opportunity to make what could be a useful point.

One key element differentiates this book from the classes I teach: obviously I cannot offer a reader of these pages feedback. Those interested in working directly with me are welcome to drop me a line at <DGSweet@aol.com>. I continue to work with students online as my schedule permits. And yes, I possess that new card of identity, a website: <www.jeffreysweet.com>. Do visit.

1
LESSON

The Power of the Unsaid Word

MARK TWAIN IS TALKING ABOUT A MAN WHO CHEATED HIM IN A business deal. The man has since died. Twain says of him, "But I bear him no malice. In fact, I'd send him a fan if I could."

If you laughed, this was probably your thought process: "Twain is contemplating sending a fan to a dead man. Why would a dead man have use for a fan? A fan is something you use to cool yourself when you're hot. Where could a dead man be that's hot?

"Oh."

Here's how Twain could have ruined his joke: "I'd send a fan to him in Hell."

What's the difference? "I'd send a fan to him in Hell" cheats the reader of the opportunity to figure out where Twain has sent this guy. The line Twain wrote allows you to be a part of the process of creating the meaning of the joke.

Grade school science teaches us that electricity needs a complete circuit in order for power to flow. When you flip on a light switch, you are putting contacts into place that create a complete circuit through which the electricity may travel. The result: the light goes on.

Similarly, when you engage the audience's ability to reason—prompting them to go through a thought process along the lines of what I charted above—you create the circumstance under which they will provide the element that completes a logical circuit. And then they see the light.

What does this have to do with writing for stage and screen?

As dramatists, we are trying to engage our audience. They are more likely to be engaged and to embrace and take to heart the meaning of a scene we have created if they are given the chance to discover that meaning for themselves. Anytime you *tell* the audience something, you deny them the opportunity to collaborate in creating that meaning. When they collaborate, they are active. When you deny them the opportunity to collaborate, they are passive and consequently have less reason to invest themselves in your material.

To embrace terms borrowed from basic logic, I think we writers should put the *premises* on the stage or screen so that the audience can come to their own *conclusions*. (Mark down those terms: *premises* and *conclusions*. I'll be coming back to them.) If Twain were to overtly tell us the man of whom he complains is in Hell, he would be stating a conclusion. If he tells us only that the man is dead and could use a fan, he is offering us the premises, leaving it to us to arrive at the conclusion regarding where the wretch is spending his afterlife.

Before I leave this joke (which, by the way, I found in his *Autobiography*), let me point out another conclusion implicit in its elegant construction. Remember, the punch line is, "But I bear him no malice. In fact, I'd send him a fan if I could." What is our evaluation of Twain's assertion, "I bear him no malice"? Since he has led us to understand that in his imagination he has boarded this guy in Hell, do we accept "I bear him no malice" at face value?

That's another way of describing a premise—face value. I suggest that much of the craft of dramatic writing is submitting face value for our audience's consideration so that they can respond by figuring out the true value for themselves.

Simply speaking, then, I think our job as dramatists is this: to create the circumstances under which actors may create compelling behavior so that the audience may have the pleasure of evaluating this behavior.

It may help if you think of the audience as detectives. In order for detectives to do their jobs, they have to have clues to link together in search of an underlying pattern of meaning. The audience, too, needs clues in order to do their job. It is up to us to offer them these clues. These clues are in the form of a script that suggests things for the actors to do.

Notice I say "to do." I believe we should be concerned less with what they are to say than what they are to do. After all, the people who perform in plays, movies, and TV shows are not called "speakers." They are called "actors" because their function is to act. Speaking is only one kind of possible action a performer may undertake. It follows that the writer's job is to provide actors with opportunities *to* act.

For their part, the audience's job is not to sit passively and appreciate our undoubted genius, but to collaborate with us. It should be our aim to stimulate them to respond to the actions we have proposed for their consideration. By making the audience our collaborators, we express a confidence and trust in them that will be repaid by their uncrossing their arms, leaning forward, and giving their full imaginative powers over to the characters and the worlds we create with them.

The first several assignments I propose are designed to help you discover how to put premises on the stage, in the reasonable confidence that your audience will arrive at appropriate conclusions.

One of my favorite examples of this technique in practice is "I've Grown Accustomed to Her Face," the song by Alan Jay Lerner and Frederick Loewe that ends *My Fair Lady*, the musical adaptation of Shaw's *Pygmalion*. In it, Higgins goes on at some length about how used to Eliza's presence he has become. There is no overt statement in which he expresses the character of his real feelings. That overt statement is not necessary. The audience translates, "I've Grown Accustomed to Her Face" to "I've Fallen in Love with Her." It's much more powerful because the audience is allowed to do the translation.

Here's an example from one of my plays. In this passage, Benny, an aging actor, faces Leo, a director and former friend who cooperated in the 1950s with the infamous House Committee on Un-American Activities by testifying he had seen Benny in the company of Communists and fellow travellers. As a result, Benny was blacklisted for years. It is now 1981. An emotional Leo has asked Benny finally—not to forgive—but to *put aside* his long-standing anger and resume the friendship. After all, as Leo says, they're going to start dying soon. Benny considers for a second and then, instead of answering directly, he says:

BENNY: Leo, you got a car?
LEO: Yeah. Why?

BENNY: Let's say for the sake of argument there's someplace you want to go. So you go to your car, put the key in the ignition—nothing. It isn't working. But there's this place you want to go. You want to go there real bad. You take a look in my garage, what do you know?—I've got a car. A car in good working condition. It's got a few years on it, but it runs fine. We're talking about a respected make. So you ask me, can you take my car? I say no, I'm sorry, I've made plans, I need it. You tell me about this place you want to go, how important it is to you to get there. I say I'm sorry, but no, I can't let you have my car. What do you do? You take it anyway. Now what do you figure I do in a situation like this? Call the cops, of course. Give them your description and the license number, they take off after you. What happens if they catch you? You end up being charged with grand theft auto. All right, you didn't steal my car. But there *was* someplace you wanted to go, and the only vehicle you could get your hands on was something else that belonged to me. Something that belonged to me, something that belonged to Morty, something that belonged to a few other guys. I don't know how you did it with them, but I get the famous phone call. You call and tell me what you're going to do. You cry about the pressure. You tell me how much getting to this place you want to go means to you. You want me to tell you, "Sure, Leo, go ahead. Take it for a drive. Barter it for the good opinion of a bunch of cynical shits. Buy yourself a license to work." But it doesn't play that way. I say no. And the next day, you go into that committee room, and you use it anyway. The difference between that and you taking my car—my car you can return.

If I have written this passage correctly, the word that should have occurred to you is "name." The tip-off is in the lines, "All right, you didn't steal my car. But there *was* someplace you wanted to go, and the only vehicle you could get your hands on was something else that belonged to me." As soon as I have Benny say "something else," the audience is invited to try to figure out what that "something else" could be. The clincher should be the last line couple of lines, "And the next day, you go into that committee room, and you use it anyway. The difference between that and you taking my car—my car you can return." I want the audience to ask, "What of Benny's could Leo have used in the committee room and, having used it, not been able to return?"

This is not an accidental effect. I knew that if I put the word "name" into that speech, I would ruin it. I want the audience to figure out the word for themselves from the context. (Admittedly, this shouldn't require much heavy lifting since the title of the play is *The Value of Names*.)

Incidentally, this technique can work on a larger level than that of an individual speech or song. When the film version of *The Godfather* was being planned, certain gentlemen of Italian background suggested to the filmmakers that the shooting might go more smoothly if the word "Mafia" weren't used in the picture. The filmmakers readily agreed. What they didn't mention was that the word "Mafia" had never been *in* the script. Given the characters and actions depicted in the film, the audience could hardly help but come up with the word on their own.

> **Assignment One:** Think of a word or a concept. Write a speech for a character or a scene in which the word or concept is never articulated but is indirectly conveyed to the audience.

By *Walt Higgins*

BILL: Remember when I came home from Vietnam, Kate?[1] I rang the bell and Mom saw me through the screen door and ran out and hugged me.[2] Dad never made it to the door. The emotion was too much for him. He collapsed in the living room. I helped him into his chair and he couldn't stop crying. He was so happy and so relieved.[3] But you just stood in the kitchen doorway looking at me like I was a stranger. Then Mom prodded you to come over to me. When you did, it wasn't real. You were just going through the motions . . . the dutiful sister.[4]

KATE: That's ridiculous, Billy. I was thrilled to see you. We all were.[5]

BILL: I never told you that I had come home earlier. I wanted to surprise Mom so I crept into the living room. You were all in the kitchen. You and Dad were arguing. I heard what you called me, Kate.[6] I sneaked out of the house and walked down to the corner and just stood in the dark, trying to figure it out. Trying to make some sense out of it. My mind just couldn't process it. But I had no place else to go so I came back and rang the bell.[7]

KATE: For Chrissakes, Billy. I was sixteen years old. It was an emotional time. The whole country was in an uproar.[8]

BILL: Over the years I convinced myself that it was just the war you were against, the uniform you were ashamed of. But then they'd find some old Nazi in Argentina and put him on trial. And it would all come back.[9]

KATE: We all said things back then that we'd like to take back.

BILL: I dreamed about coming home for a year. Every day the dream got bigger, better, more perfect. Sometimes I still dream about how it's gonna be, or should have been.

KATE: It's been thirty years, Billy. Are you going to hold one stupid remark against me for the rest of my life?

BILL: I could deal with Pete and Debbie crossing the street when they saw me in uniform. They weren't family. And that arrogant philosophy professor at Manhattan College who refused to teach Vietnam vets. They kicked his ass out. But you were my kid sister. God, I wish we could go back to the way it was before that. I wish we could go back and make it right.[10]

1. Not that I'd lay out a rule that one should never do this or that, but speeches that begin "remember when" tend to signal sleepy-time for an audience. A memory speech should be motivated in the needs of the moment—the person articulating the memory has to be trying to get something here and now by saying this. Even when you write a speech in the past tense, the *action* of the scene must be in the present tense, or else the audience suspects that the reason the speech is there is that you, the author, are trying to sneak in some info.

2. I find that often, once one has introduced the idea that the speaker is recounting a story from the past, it's useful to switch to something known as the historical present. The implication is that the narrator is getting so caught up in the immediacy of the memories that, instead of recounting something that's done and gone, the teller is virtually reporting on images appearing now in the mind's eye. Take, for instance, your line: "I rang the bell and Mom saw me through the

screen door and ran out and hugged me." I think this would be more effective as: "I ring the bell and Mom sees me through the screen door and runs out and hugs me." As I will discuss at greater length later, I believe dialogue works best when written in the present and future tenses. I suggest you take a look at any past-tense speech and see if it's possible to switch it to the present so as to gain an impression of greater immediacy.

3. "The emotion was too much for him" is a line that states a conclusion. You write, "Dad doesn't make it to the door. He collapses in the living room. I help him to his chair and he can't stop crying." This is all the audience needs to figure out that the emotion is too much for him. Nor do you need "so happy and so relieved." The audience is smart enough to know that the return of a son from the Vietnam War in one piece is likely to trigger feelings of happiness and relief.

4. Again, I think this could be done more effectively if it were a little less direct, without "like a stranger," "it wasn't real," "going through the motions," and "dutiful sister." These are all evaluations, conclusions. They state the truth and so leave the audience no room to figure anything out.

   On the fly, this is the kind of thing I might do as an alternative: "But you just stand in the kitchen doorway. You look at me, then you look at Mom like, 'What am I supposed to do?' She prods you over to me. Do you hug me? You put out your hand, 'pleased to meet you' almost, except maybe 'pleased' isn't the word. Like you have a checklist of etiquette for the occasion to guide you through, only someone slipped you the wrong list." I don't claim that this is brilliant, but the audience would interpret this and arrive at most of the conclusions you desire.

5. So why am I not giving you grief for "ridiculous" and "thrilled to see you"? Because the audience is going to come to different conclusions than that this is ridiculous and that she was thrilled to see him. Evaluative words can be useful when the audience believes them to be *inaccurate*. The audience thinks, "That's not true," and then comes up with its own idea of what is true. In *My Fair Lady*, Higgins sings, "I'm an ordinary man," and the audience is united in thinking, "bullshit."

6. Good! Now you pique my curiosity. I lean forward wanting to know what it was she said.

7. Here again I think an indirect approach would work. I don't think you need, "My mind just couldn't process it." I think you could get what you need with, "I start thinking about where else I could stay. Friends with a spare couch, maybe an old girlfriend who'd say yes for old times' sake. But I can't come up with anything, so I go back and ring the bell." By having him talk about a problem he was trying to solve, you raise in the audience's mind the issue of why he had this problem. I think the viewer would come up with: "He wouldn't be looking for a different place to stay if he didn't feel uncomfortable or unwelcome in his own house because of what he overheard Kate saying."

8. Again, there's a less direct and, I think, more effective way. Here's my suggestion:

> **KATE:** How old was I?
>
> **BILLY:** What does that have to do with—?
>
> **KATE:** How old? It was June 1970. I was born in March 1954. Do the math.
>
> **BILLY:** All right.
>
> **KATE:** And do you remember what happened in May 1970? Do the words "Kent State" ring any bells?

9. "And it would all come back." I think this is where you play off your earlier image. "And what you said in the kitchen would come back—the words you used." And the audience would be invited a second time (particularly with the Nazi reference) to figure out what the words are.

10. I'm not going to go over every other word in the scene. But, despite my picking, I think this does indeed answer the assignment. The unspoken words are "war criminal," and they have more power because we get to figure them out. What I'm suggesting with these other comments is that it's possible to use this same idea—the power of what is left unsaid—throughout a passage, rather than just for one idea.

By Jeanine Barone

A Monologue

Your behavior is no better than what goes on in the rest of the animal kingdom. Sure, there are plenty of animals that are designed to mimic some other, usually deadly, creatures but that doesn't make it right. Unlike the rest of us, they don't have a choice. And it only works for them because it helps them escape predators. Those fish that have a dot at the end of their tail must think they're pretty sly when a predator mistakes it for a big eye. And that butterfly who has the same exact color pattern as its very nasty-tasting cousin gets away without so much as a nibble. What's unbelievable is that plants, which seem on the surface so innocent, are no better, mimicking the color of more toxic, look-alike species. But, I'd like it a whole lot better if they all just showed us their true colors. Yeah, I know they risk getting eaten, but maybe if there was that risk they'd spend just a little more time actively protecting themselves instead of depending on their little charade. And what's really sad is that they obviously have to maintain their little ruse among their own kind as well.

The unspoken word here is, of course, "camouflage." And yes, the speech's effectiveness is based on that word being unspoken. The only comment I want to make at this point is something that I will probably make a number of times: I believe it is best to avoid adjectives that involve moral evaluations. This isn't to say that we shouldn't deal with moral issues, but—consistent with the premises-and-conclusions concept—these issues tend to be most effectively invoked when the evaluation isn't in the text but occurs in the audience's mind. So "your behavior is no better" and "that doesn't make it right" would be more effective if the audience came up with these thoughts themselves. ("Ah, this character doesn't think that the person being addressed is any better than an animal, isn't behaving well.") I like the details about the fish and butterfly's markings and, generally, I think your use of indirection by talking about animals as opposed to humans works well.

SIDEBAR 1

The Present Tense

THORNTON WILDER WAS ONE OF THE RARE WRITERS WHO WAS A success as both a dramatist and a novelist (he won the Pulitzer Prize both for playwriting and fiction), and he gave serious thought to the differences between these two crafts. He articulated some of his theories in a terse and valuable essay called "Some Thoughts on Playwriting," which appeared in an anthology called *Playwrights on Playwriting* (edited by Toby Cole). In it, he wrote, "A play visibly represents pure existing. A novel is what one mind, claiming to omniscience, asserts to have existed." That is to say, a play is about now, and a novel, usually, is about then.

Though a relative handful of novels are composed in the present tense, for the most part, as Wilder notes, fiction is written in the past tense. When Dickens begins A *Tale of Two Cities* with, "It was the best of times, it was the worst of times," he is establishing the voice of a narrator getting ready to tell us something that occurred in those particular times. This is a common practice in the first chapter of a novel, to establish when in the past—whether last night or centuries before—the story being told is set.

On the other hand, scripts—whether for stage or screen—describe something that is happening *now*. (In fact, they are not so much descriptions as prescriptions—telling the actors what actions to take.) Oscar throws the pasta against the wall (*The Odd Couple*), Margaret places the paper crown on York's head (*Henry VI, Part 3*), Norman tries to seduce his sisters-in-law (*The Norman Conquests*), Regina allows her husband to die on the stairs (*The Little Foxes*). These are all actions the audience witnesses. A script is an account of such actions, of what the writer intends to unfold moment-by-moment in the presence of those who have bought tickets.

Because plays and movies deal in present-tense action, I think the most effective dialogue tends also to be in the present tense. As I wrote in Lesson 1, I tend to be wary of speeches that begin, "I remember . . ." You can almost feel the energy seep out of a scene when a character says, "I remember." The audience knows from experience that what follows is likely to be a passage that will explain prior circumstances.

I don't like explanations. I think they are mostly antidramatic.

The audience is watching to see what characters will decide to do. Decisions are made in the present, though some decisions are about how one hopes to meet the future. Obviously decisions can't be made about how to behave in the past. The time to make those decisions is long gone. Yes, one can make a decision about how to *interpret* the past, but that decision is a present-tense one, it doesn't change the actions that have already been taken.

I think that this preference for keeping to the present applies to writing for actors no matter the medium. Plays, movies, or TV programs that start with a lot of talk about the past risk trying the audience's patience. But, of course, there's the impulse to get that old devil exposition in. And the exposition is usually about what happened prior to the action your script is going to depict, which tends to drag you to the past.

I believe you can get the necessary info out without relying too much on the past. I believe it's more important to create vivid, present-tense negotiations—especially early in the script—in order to stimulate the audience's curiosity about the past. Much of this book deals with various techniques for doing this.

I'm not saying there aren't some stunning passages written in the past tense. The major arias in Eugene O'Neill's *Long Day's Journey into Night* describe what has gone before. And so does the famous scene (reportedly written by John Milius) in the film version of *Jaws* in which Quint talks about having been a member of the crew of the U.S.S. Indianapolis, and what befell the survivors of a torpedo attack in shark-infested waters. Where do these scenes fall in their respective scripts? In the last thirds. We've seen so much of these characters earlier in present-tense scenes that we have enough invested in them to be willing to follow them into their pasts.

So, no, you don't have to begin a script articulating what brought the characters to this moment. You can start them off *in* the moment. I reprint an example from the way I begin *Flyovers*. The scene is a deck in a suburban backyard. At rise, we meet Ted and Oliver, both in their forties. They're both dressed casually, but, in contrast to Oliver's tasteful getup, Ted's clothes come from K-Mart.

TED: You really get into it sometimes, the two of you. You and, uh—

OLIVER: Sarah.

TED: Sarah, yeah. Sometimes you seem to be really—

OLIVER: Well, that's part of the fun of it.

TED: —really pissed at each other.

OLIVER: No, not pissed.

TED: She doesn't tick you off? Her attitude: "Of course you'd like that piece of crap, Oliver, it's got explosions and butts and boobs. Cuz you're a guy." That doesn't make you—

OLIVER: That's part of the act.

TED: The act? You mean it's a phony?

OLIVER: No, the opinions we have are the opinions we have. But the idea of the show—the thing that makes our show different from Siskel and Ebert or those other guys—is that it's a man and a woman. The idea—the way we sold it to the syndicator—was a lot of couples go to the movies together—

["Sold" is the first past-tense verb in the scene.]

TED: I think they call those "dates."

OLIVER: —and they end up talking about the same kind of stuff, issues, we get into on—

TED: So you're, what?—representing these couples?

OLIVER: Sort of.

TED: She's talking about the movie from, like, the woman's point of view, and you're doing it from the guy's?

OLIVER: More or less.

TED: So you're supposed to be the male point of view. What? Representing?

OLIVER: Pretty much.

TED: Representing, for instance, me?

OLIVER: You?

TED: I'm a male. I have a male point of view.

OLIVER: You put it that way—

TED: Hunh. You like movies with subtitles, right?

OLIVER: I like some of them.

TED: I like none of them. So right there, you don't represent me. You don't speak for my male point of view.

OLIVER: I don't have your confidence.

TED: Not when it comes to movies.

OLIVER: Well, no two people are going to have the same taste, the same perspective.

TED: But my bet is that you and that woman—

OLIVER: Sarah.

TED: —yeah, see more eye-to-eye about movies than you and me would. That the two of you would probably agree with each other more often about what is or isn't a shitty movie than you and me. This, despite the fact that you and me, we're both guys, which is something you and she don't have in common.

OLIVER: Your point?

TED: I think I just said it.

[Past tense, referring to an action in the immediate past.]

OLIVER: I guess I missed—

[Immediate past again.]

TED: You and her—a man and a woman—have more in common than you and me, who are two guys. But you'd normally think it would be the two guys who have more in common.

OLIVER: That's the point you're making?

TED: Yes. That's my point.

OLIVER: Fair enough.

I think the scene is specific and urgent because it stays in the present.

After a few pages of this, then I feel I can relax a bit and deal a bit more about the history of their relationship. But the bulk of the script—the overwhelming majority of it—is written very purposefully in the present tense, and I think that's why it feels so immediate when it plays.

2
LESSON

Negotiation Over Objects

THE USE OF PREMISES AND CONCLUSIONS EXTENDS BEYOND leaving a word unsaid.

By way of example, let me quote a little more from *Flyovers*. Oliver, a middle-aged New Yorker who appears on TV as an entertainment journalist, is visiting the struggling Midwestern town where he went to high school. At this point in the action, he is having a drink on the back deck of Ted's home. When they were teens, Ted used to thrash Oliver with numbing regularity, but now Ted is making a serious effort to be agreeable to his successful former classmate. The two have been joined by Iris, who also went to high school with them and for whom Oliver once had an unrequited and unarticulated crush. Shortly before the passage below, Oliver has received a call on his cell phone from his New York office. Now he takes an electronic organizer out of his pocket and begins to type information into it, prompting an observation from Ted.

TED: You're a walking electronics outlet—The cell phone, this—

OLIVER: It's how I keep my schedule straight. And, you know, appointments and addresses and phone numbers.

TED: How many numbers can it hold?

OLIVER: A few thousand, I guess.

TED: You know that many people?

OLIVER: I didn't say I filled it all.

TED: Put me in there. Me and Iris. We want to be in your organizer.

IRIS: Speak for yourself.

TED: You don't want to be in Oliver's organizer? You too good to be in Oliver's—

IRIS: Oliver hasn't invited me to be in his organizer.

OLIVER: You want to be in my organizer?

IRIS: OK now—

OLIVER: McCarty, right? Iris McCarty?

IRIS: You don't have to.

OLIVER: Let me just get to the M's.
 (He *fiddles with the keyboard.*)

IRIS: It's really—

OLIVER: No, I think it—There we go. McCarty. M.C. not M.A.C., right?

IRIS: Right.

OLIVER: Here.
 (He *offers it to her.*)

IRIS: I should type it in?

OLIVER: Why not?

IRIS: All right.
 (She *starts typing her particulars in.*)
What do I do now?

OLIVER: Just hit "save." Right there, see?
 (She *does it.*)

TED: My turn, my turn!
 (Ted *grabs the organizer.*)
Jeez, you need fingers like, what's his name, the guy from *Fantasy Island*? "The plane, the plane!"

OLIVER: If you want me to type it—

TED: No, I can do it.
 (He *types.*)
Well, I guess this is possible.

OLIVER: I wouldn't want to write a long article on it.

TED (Pressing a button): Save.
 (Ted *doesn't hand it back to Oliver.*)

So, who we in there with?

OLIVER: Oh—my accountant. The liquor store. Joan Callahan, my producer. . . . .

TED: John Travolta?

OLIVER: No.

TED: If I look under "T" in here, I wouldn't find John Travolta's home number?

OLIVER: No.

TED: But there *are* famous people in here. People I've heard of.

OLIVER: Mostly their offices. Maybe their managers.

TED: How do you like that, Iris? We're in the same organizer as some famous people's managers.

IRIS: You want to give that back to him?

TED: I'm sorry, of course.
(*Hands it back to Oliver.*)

Even though Ted is making seeming gestures of conciliation toward Oliver, his envy of Oliver's success leads him to taunt Oliver with an object associated with that success—the organizer. By having Oliver take up the idea of putting Iris' name into the organizer, I also suggest that Oliver's interest in her is still alive. In addition, the passage fills in a bit more of the world in which Oliver moves and his desire to appear modest.

If I have written this scene correctly, the audience will get all of this as a by-product of the introduction of Oliver's organizer and Ted's commandeering of it.

My point: you can stimulate the audience to come to the conclusions you intend through the way you have your characters handle or negotiate over a well-selected object.

Assignment Two: Choose a physical object and write a short scene in which we find out who two characters are through the way they negotiate over that object. Don't allow the characters to explain themselves. Don't let them go into a lot of blather about their pasts. Have them deal with the here and now and the disposition of the object you've selected.

By Jeannine M. Saunders

(A living room. Travis is resting on his couch. He has a cast on one leg, from his toes to mid-calf. The room is cluttered with magazines, books, and other miscellany. Fast food wrappers and cups litter the coffee table. Travis is flipping through TV channels with the remote control when his wife, Lisa, enters, carrying a bag.)

TRAVIS: This is ridiculous!

(He slams down the remote on the coffee table.)

LISA: What is?

TRAVIS: This so-called cable! Fifty dollars a month for 68 channels filled with infomercials and talk shows![1]

(He picks up the remote again and clicks it.)

Even ESPN. Look! It's some has-been TV wrestler, trying to sell me a goddamned exercise machine.

(He throws down the remote again and it slides across the table.)

LISA *(Sitting down in a chair near him)*: It's not the remote's fault.[2]

TRAVIS: I didn't hurt it.

(He leans up to reach for it and cringes.)

Oww! Shit! That was nice. Did you get my medicine?

(She hands him the bag, which he opens. He pulls out a bottle of medicine and reads the label.)

What is this? Ten tablets? This isn't going to last me a week! Are you sure they got this right?

LISA: It's what the doctor called in.

(He picks up the remote and flips through a few channels. Lisa stays where she is and stares at the TV. He turns his head and stares at her until she looks at him.)

What?

TRAVIS: Water? If you could manage it?[3]

(She shakes her head, gets up and exits. He continues to flip through channels, puts down the remote, picks up a magazine, pages through it and then tosses it on the table as Lisa comes back in with a glass of water. She hands it to him.)

Appreciate it.

(*She sits down and he opens the bottle and shakes out two pills which he swallows with the water.*)

LISA: What are you doing? You're only supposed to take one.[4]

TRAVIS: Well, it hurts enough for two. They're not that strong.

(*He goes for the remote one more time and still finds nothing to watch. He throws the remote on the floor.*)

Goddammit!

LISA (*Picking up the remote*): I'll bet that'll teach it, huh?

TRAVIS: I'm going to go nuts before this is over with!

LISA: There're other things to do besides watch TV.

TRAVIS: What?

LISA: I don't know—

TRAVIS: Come on. You're the creative one in the family. Come up with something entertaining.

LISA: No—

TRAVIS: Hey, you brought it up.

LISA: It's not that hard. We could . . . listen to some music or get out the Trivial Pursuit game—

TRAVIS: I hate that game—

LISA: We could talk about our day.

TRAVIS: Yeah, right. Okay, I got up, got on the couch, slept, ordered in pizza, ate, took a piss, slept, and watched . . . *tried* to watch TV. How about you?

LISA: You really what to know?

TRAVIS: Sure.

LISA: Okay. Well, at lunch I ran down to the Farmer's Market, that new place in old town. It's so quaint! Anyway, I found this one lady who has a booth—

(*Travis's eye is caught by the TV and he begins to watch.*)

—and she sells paintings on consignment. Good ones, too. So I talked to her and she said—

(*She notices that he is watching TV.*)

—and she said she'd let me—

25

(He chuckles at the TV.)

—let me screw every starving artist in the county.[5]

(He gives her no response.)

TRAVIS!

TRAVIS: Huh? Oh, I'm sorry, babe. The dope's kicking in. And look, it's *Dragnet*. I haven't seen this in years.

(She stares at him for a minute. Then picks up the remote control. She points it at him and clicks it several times.)

LISA: I think it is broken.

(She drops the remote on the table and leaves the room.)

The main object in this scene, of course, is the channel changer. One of the things I like about the way it's used is that it is established as being an object associated with him, and she ends up taking it and using it for other purposes. As in my scene from *Flyovers*, the appropriation of another person's property offers a useful dramatic payoff. Specific notes:

1. You don't need the first two lines. The scene starts more strongly if he is in the middle of complaining about specifics than if he begins with the evaluation, "This is ridiculous." From his complaint, we'll figure out that he thinks this is ridiculous. I also think that the line, "This so-called cable!" is not needed. "Fifty dollars a month for infomercials and talk shows" establishes the idea. Anybody who has cable or has been exposed to it—which is to say almost everybody—will know what the line means and what his complaint is.

2. Frequently it's more useful to have characters say the opposite of what they mean. Perhaps instead of, "It's not the remote's fault," it might be more effective if she said, "Yeah, it's the remote's fault." In general, avoid having characters say the obvious. The audience will have already anticipated the obvious. The idea is to delight the audience by improving on what they expect.

3. Again, with the issue of the water, you're effectively using the negotiation-over-objects principle. His line, "Water? If you could manage it?" certainly nails his gratuitous hostility.

4. The fact that he takes two pills instead of one is again a useful

object-based negotiation. This establishes that he is headstrong to the point of possible self-endangerment. But you don't need the line, "What are you doing?" When I interviewed Alan Arkin for *Something Wonderful Right Away*, he said that one of the things he learned working at Second City was that an improvisation is likely to fail if one actor establishes an activity and a second comes in and, instead of joining the activity, says, "What are you doing?" Arkin observed, "You know that's the end. There's no possible way that scene is going to work because all you'll get is an explanation of what the first guy is doing while the second guy makes cracks about the first guy's activity." The converse is true—a scene will often get a healthy start if the second character enters and joins the activity established by the first, even if they don't talk about the activity at all but, as they cooperate, deal with another issue entirely.

5. There are some devices that are now so familiar that they have outlived their usefulness. I think having someone say something outrageous (frequently sexual) without it being noticed by the other person in the scene is a bit that has been done too many times to have much punch left.

One of the things I'm left wondering at the end of this piece is what Travis is like when he is not in pain and miserable. Is he mean all the time or just because of his present circumstances? It would be interesting if there were the occasional suggestion of just what has kept these two people together. Presumably this is not the complete picture of their relationship, there are or have been other aspects.

By *Mike Donohue*

INT. BATHROOM. DAY.

MARK BENZO reaches around the shower curtain for a bath mat. Finding none, he steps out of the shower, dripping wet, puddling onto the bare floor, stretches for the flowery pink towel on the rack over the toilet, and wraps the towel around his waist.[1] The steam from the shower has fogged the mirror. Mark gropes across the cluttered counter for his glasses. They are fogged too.

MARK

Jesus, Tina, what's wrong with the fan?

TINA (O.S.)

Gotta turn it on, baby.

Mark gropes along the wall and finds a switch. The room goes dark.

MARK

Shit.[2]

Sound of fan.

MARK (Cont.)

I got it. I got it.

Mark switches the light on. He squints, trying to see himself in the mirror. He swipes ineffectually at the fog on the mirror and still can't see anything.

TINA (V.O.)

Use my blow dryer.

MARK

The what?

TINA enters the bathroom without knocking.[3] She looks at the puddles on the floor, frowns, then gets a blow dryer from a drawer under the sink, plugs it in and blows a clear spot on the foggy mirror. Mark takes it from her. Sparks shoot from the blow dryer and it stops working. Mark hits it a couple of times, then sets it down warily.

TINA

Men. Better shave, baby. You got a face like a bear's behind.[4]

MARK

Razor?

Tina reaches into the top drawer and extracts an ancient, worn, plastic women's razor. She hands it to Mark, who stands holding it, looking at it in disbelief.[5]

MARK (Cont.)

What the hell am I supposed to do with this?

Tina pats him on the cheek.

TINA

I think Tina's big, strong man can figure that out.

Tina leaves the bathroom. Mark uses the bar soap to lather up his face. He scrapes the razor painfully down his cheek. Blood spurts from an inch-long cut.

MARK

Ow-wah!

He reaches down for toilet paper, yanking on the end, the paper unrolling endlessly around his feet. He rips off a corner of the paper and dabs it onto the cut. It immediately fills with blood.

MARK (Cont.)

Maybe I can tell Moira I was slashed by a mugger.[6]

TINA (O.S.)

What, baby?

MARK

Nothing.

Mark opens the medicine cabinet and sees row upon row of pill bottles. Behind them he spots the toothpaste and reaches for it, knocking the pill bottles into the sink.

MARK (Cont.)
Shit, shit, shit. What the hell do you need all these pills for?

TINA (O.S.)
I don't take pills.

MARK
I've got a sink full of this crap that says you're wrong.

Mark picks up a pill bottle, squints and holds it close enough to see. He picks up another, and another.

MARK (Cont.)
Jesus, Tina, these things are so far out of date they ought to be in the Smithsonian.[7]

He dumps all of the pill bottles into a plastic wastebasket he finds under the sink. He takes the toothpaste, looks around for a toothbrush, doesn't find one, squirts some toothpaste on his index finger and begins to brush his teeth.[8]

TINA (O.S.)
Except for the birth control pills. But I haven't taken those since July.

Tina giggles. Mark sprays toothpaste onto the mirror and stiffens in wide-eyed shock. He puts on a robe, hers, pulls his fogged glasses on, and throws open the bathroom door. Tina is applying lipstick at a mirror.

TINA
I told you I had my tubes tied, didn't I?

Mark turns back into the bathroom and closes the door.

This nails the assignment cold. Terrific use of objects to reveal the nature of the relationship between Mark and Tina. Let me get specific:

1. The flowery pink towel would tip us off that he's probably not at home. While this is something that might not be as easy to pick up onstage, on film it will be very vivid.

2. This reinforces the idea that he's not on home turf. Not only not on home turf, but fairly unfamiliar with this turf, which would imply that this is a new relationship. This is almost certainly the first time he's been in her apartment.

3. Her walking in without knocking is a vivid way of showing what her standard of privacy is, and hinting that it might be different from his. Especially if he instinctively covers up when she comes in.

4. Tina's language is zippy and colloquial. I wouldn't be surprised if she were younger than Mark, though, of course, this is something you could establish in the description introducing her.

5. I very much like her handing him the plastic women's razor. It suggests that his visit there was unanticipated by either of them. Also, there is a nice sense that his masculine self-image is nicked by shaving with something that's probably made out of pink plastic.

6. Ah, Moira! First hint that he's cheating. He's probably either married or in a long-term relationship.

7. The idea that something's so old that it belongs in the Smithsonian is a cliché and should be avoided. Another one to avoid: "So-and-so looked like a deer caught in the headlights." Whatever freshness the simile once held has now been worn down by overuse. I recently heard a quote: "A cliché is something somebody has said before." (Does my quoting it make it a cliché?) I don't go quite that far, but if you have the opportunity to mint some new phrases, why not seize it?

8. His knocking stuff over, putting toothpaste on his finger, etc., all underscore how out of his normal element he is. It also implies that he and Tina may not be—uh—an appropriate match? She is blithe and dismissive of things that concern him seriously.

There's no heavy-handed exposition, no explaining endlessly stuff that the people would already know. Yet, by the way they handle these objects, we're coming to a working hypothesis of the nature of their relationship. We know it's a new relationship, we get hints of the difference in their values, and we get some idea that, from his perspective, this is an illicit situation. Also that this is probably a new relationship. Very smart work.

3
LESSON

Misuse, Transformation,
or Destruction of an Object

OBJECTS ARE NOT ALWAYS USED FOR THE PURPOSES FOR WHICH they were intended.

In Billy Wilder and I. A. L. Diamond's screenplay for *The Apartment*, C. C. Baxter (Jack Lemmon)—clowning to amuse a depressed guest—uses his tennis racket to make pasta, demonstrating its applicability both to straining spaghetti and serving meatballs.

At the end of *The Graduate* (directed by Mike Nichols, from a screenplay credited to Calder Willingham and Buck Henry), Benjamin, rescuing Elaine from a loveless marriage, grabs a big cross from a stand in the church and swings it at the wedding guests to keep them from charging. When he and Elaine emerge from the building, to prevent pursuit, he uses the cross again, jamming closed the church doors.

In both of these movies, the filmmakers not only made the characters' relationships to other characters vivid through the use of an object, they jolted the audience by transforming that object so it could perform a new and unanticipated function.

Transformation often involves using a high-status object for a low-status purpose (or vice versa), further violating the audience's expectation. The cross in *The Graduate* is a very high-status object, and part of the scene's power lies in an object with religious meaning being used first as a crude weapon and then a barricade.

During an interview with director Paul Sills, I asked for his opinion on the practice of using improvisational techniques to create TV commercials. His response was that doing so was like using a diamond to stop a bottle. Damn good simile, and one that makes its point by the hypothetical transformation of a valuable jewel to a purpose that could be accomplished by a dime-store gadget.

Comics often subvert the usual functions of props. Jonathan Winters established his resourcefulness by approaching a table full of objects and using a mixing bowl, say, as a football helmet or a banana as a telephone. Robin Williams (who is the first to acknowledge Winters' influence on him) has also made this a frequent feature of his performances, and often the players on the TV series *Whose Line Is It Anyway?* are similarly asked by the host to improvise short scenes based on the ingenious misuse of props.

This is hardly a new idea, of course. In *The Second Shepherds' Play*, a thief, hoping to elude discovery, wraps the lamb he has stolen in swaddling clothes, puts it into a cradle and tries to pass it off to pursuing shepherds as his baby. In *The Gold Rush*, Charlie Chaplin sticks forks into two dinner rolls, creating the illusion of a pair of small legs, and, with his head hovering above, plays with the forks to suggest dancing. In *South Pacific* (by Richard Rodgers, Oscar Hammerstein II, and Joshua Logan), the character Luther Billis, in drag for the number "Honey-Bun," wears "two coconut shells on his chest to simulate 'femininity.'" When a fellow serviceman lifts up one of the coconuts, it turns out that it serves another purpose— as a hiding place for his smokes. So the coconuts are transformed into a bra, and the bra is further transformed into a stash for cigarettes.

Transformation is at the very heart of the theatre. "Let us . . . on your imaginary forces work," Shakespeare has the Chorus say at the beginning of *Henry V*. He further announces that, with our collaboration, he intends to transform actors into royalty ("your thoughts . . . now must deck our kings"), make the beginning of a new scene suggest a move to a new location perhaps miles from the location of the scene it succeeds ("Carry them here and there"), and telescope time ("Turning th' accomplishment of many years/Into an hour-glass . . .").

We are in the habit of accepting the Chorus' bargain whenever we go to the theatre. We watch *Peter Pan* knowing that the ever-young boy is (usually) being played by a woman and that his flying is done with wires. We know, too, that Tinker Bell is a combination of a pin spot and a percussionist in the orchestra playing a celeste. We know these things to be literally true, yet we agree to engage our imaginations to transform these literal elements into a boy who can fly and his very tiny, very jealous friend.

For her adaptation of Ovid's *Metamorphosis* (for Chicago's Lookingglass Theatre), writer-director Mary Zimmerman and set designer Dan Ostling constructed a large pool filled with water almost knee-deep. A broad wooden frame surrounded the pool. Upstage, to the left, they placed a large door. At one point in the story, a man undertook an ocean voyage. This is how Zimmerman staged it: His wife stood in front of the door waving. Standing downstage and to the side of her, in the middle of the pool, the husband faced her. Seated behind him on the frame, three actors with oars mimed rowing in the galley. Meanwhile, in another area of the pool, another cast member slowly pulled across the water a model of a boat. We in the audience had no trouble translating these elements into one coherent image. We completed the image in our head out of the pieces that Zimmerman offered us.

This points to one of the key differences between stage and film: no matter how realistic the setting and staging of a play, this element of transformation applies; when you go to the theatre, you have to agree to translate in your imagination the elements on the stage into what they are intended to represent. In film, though technical gimmickery is employed, the idea is to persuade you that you are seeing a recording of something that is real, even if what is represented is palpably preposterous.

Back to the subject of transforming objects: there is no more radical way you can transform something than to destroy it. In *Mad Forest*, that fearless playwright Caryl Churchill demonstrates the power of destruction by beginning the first scene with a series of nonverbal negotiations over objects culminating in a small but shocking act of violence.

The setting is the apartment of the Vladu family living in Romania under the Ceausescu regime. At the scene's start, Bogdan and his wife Irina—both smoking Romanian cigarettes—glower at each other while music plays on their radio. Suddenly Bogdan cranks up the volume of the radio and they begin to yell at each other. We can't hear a word of their argument because of the loudness of the music. Then two young women who are evidently their daughters enter, laughing. They stop laughing when they see the expressions on their parents' faces. The mother turns the radio back down.

The two young women have brought goodies—four eggs and some American cigarettes. Irina stubs out her Romanian smoke in favor of an American one. Bogdan insists on finishing his Romanian cigarette before reluctantly succumbing to the temptation of the American brand offered to him. Then, having lit up, Bogdan quite deliberately picks up one of the four eggs and drops it. After a moment of shock, Irina takes the other three eggs out of Bogdan's reach. Finally, Florina, one of the daughters, "gets a cup and spoon and scrapes up what she can of the egg off the floor." The other daughter, Lucia, doesn't move.

Not a single line is spoken in this astonishing passage, but look at how much is dramatized:

We have a strong sense of the paranoia of the society in which they live by virtue of the family saying nothing except when they crank the volume of the radio up so high as to frustrate possible eavesdroppers. We can glean the state of the Romanian economy through the value the family places on eggs and American cigarettes. We further infer that the daughters have acquired these on the black market.

We also have a fair amount of information about the politics between the members of the family—the state of hostility between Bogdan and Irina (their screamfest while the radio is blaring), the desire on the part of the daughters to repair the breach with their father (the offer of the cigarette), Bogdan's strain of self-destructive anger (the dropping of the egg), and the women's adaptation to the unpleasant situation (Irina rescuing the remaining eggs and Florina salvaging the remains of the dropped one). We have learned all this without Churchill resorting to dialogue. Even though Churchill has provided not a single spoken word, this is playwriting of an extremely high order. When Bogdan drops that egg, the audience gasps.

Shakespeare employs transformation alternatively to move us, to make us laugh, and to make us shudder. At the end of *The Winter's Tale*, what seems to be a statue of Hermione is transformed into a living, breathing person, the climax of one of the most moving reconciliation scenes in theatre. In A *Midsummer Night's Dream*, Oberon substitutes a donkey's head for Bottom's usual mug, then bewitches Titania so that she will become infatuated with this unlikely object of affection. In *Titus Andronicus*, Titus invites his enemy Tamora to dinner; after she has taken a bite or two out of the pies he's placed before her, he reveals that the meat in them is derived from the bodies of her slaughtered sons.

Movies are filled with breathtaking transformations. Many of the big special effects pictures—such as *Independence Day*, *Armageddon*, *Godzilla*, and the two *Ghostbusters* films—give the audience a special charge by turning familiar cityscapes into rubble. A large part of the appeal of the saga of the sinking of the Titanic is the transformation of a seemingly secure world (echoing the social order on land) into a huge sinking trap. What was down is now up, what was safe is now perilous. And how movies love explosions!—turning elegant cars into junk heaps, palaces of privilege and power into smoking ruins, and pursuing helicopters equipped with machine guns into fireballs.

Horror films and comedies, too, employ transformations to great effect. Once upon a time, when Lon Chaney Jr. shape-shifted from a normal-looking guy into the Wolf Man, the shift was accomplished with fake-looking fades from Chaney without fur to Chaney with. (The ominous music helped, too.) These days, computer geniuses have come up with a technique called morphing that makes impossible transformations appear seamless. In *The Mask* and *The Nutty Professor*, much of the humor comes from Jim Carrey and Eddie Murphy going from normal (well, relatively normal) human beings to characters with the surreal plasticity of cartoon figures. The technology involved may be more intricate, but when Jeff Goldblum blows up a seemingly invincible alien space ship, he's not doing something all that different from the Gentleman Caller accidentally knocking over Laura's statue of a unicorn in *The Glass Menagerie*.

The transformation of objects is a technique Melissa Manchester and I used several times in I *Sent a Letter to My Love*, a musical we cowrote based on the novel of the same name by Bernice Rubens.

The piece concerns a sister and brother in their late forties named Amy and Stan, who live together in a house by a lake in a small town in the 1950s. Stan had polio as a boy and is confined to a wheelchair. Amy has been caring for him all of her life. Neither of them has ever married. In fact, when a shy and nervous woman named Gwen comes to talk to them about renting a cottage on their property, Gwen assumes that they are wife and husband. Amy corrects this impression quickly:

AMY: He's not my husband.

GWEN: I'm sorry. I didn't mean to pry.

AMY: No, he's not my *that* either. He's my brother.

STAN: You thought we were married?

GWEN: I assumed.

STAN (*Amused*): She thought we were married.

AMY (*Hiding irritation*): Yes, well we thought *she* was married.

STAN: So we're all footloose and fancy-free.

(*Gwen begins to sneeze. She holds up her hand.*)

GWEN: Excuse me for a—

(*Gwen starts rooting around in her purse. In so doing, she knocks it over and everything falls out.*)

Oh my—

(*Amy leans down to help. She picks up a small bottle.*)

AMY: Smelling salts?

GWEN: Uh yes, sometimes I have—It usually passes very quickly. You must think I'm so clumsy. I promise I won't destroy your cottage.

Gwen knocking over her purse gives visual expression to her discomfort. The purse's upset helps convey the degree to which she herself is upset. Amy's discovery of the smelling salts among the strewn contents also helps characterize Gwen. The fact that Gwen carries them with her suggests that she is both prone to dizzy spells and old-fashioned about the solution. The scene also transforms the assumption that, till this point in the script, Gwen (and the audience) have had that Amy and Stan are a married couple by making clear that they are in fact sister and brother.

As the story continues, Amy and Stan decide to allow Gwen to rent the cottage, and the three become close. Gwen is a repressed soul who has had no romance in her life. Nor has either she or Amy ever been so bold as to wear pants. Then, one day, both women appear for a picnic dressed in slacks. Stan is delighted, and the three of them go out for a day's romp.

Stan has been corresponding with a lady named Angela, for whom he harbors romantic hopes. In a letter to Angela, Stan tells how Gwen's pants ripped when she was horsing around with Amy giving him a quick view of something pink underneath. The ripping of the pants (which is in Rubens' original novel) of course has sexual connotations. It suggests that Gwen's inhibitions are giving way, and Stan's delighted reaction foreshadows what is to happen between them.

As the audience discovers, unbeknown to Stan, the "Angela" to whom Stan is sending these letters of increasing ardor is, in fact, his sister Amy writing under that pseudonym. (I won't stop now to explain how this comes to pass.) The correspondence between Stan and "Angela" gets rather hot. Toward the end of the show, when Stan and Gwen decide to marry, Amy realizes that the wisest action for her is to dispose of her copies of the letters so that Stan will never stumble on them and find out his passionate correspondent was his own sister. Alone in the kitchen with the letters, she decides on a course of action.

AMY: Matches.

> (*She begins to look through the drawers. Stan appears in the doorway.*)

STAN: Forgot my hat.

> (*She looks up, startled, holding a box of matches. Stan moves forward, takes his hat off the table. He sees the letters. A beat.*)

You're going to burn something?

AMY: Stan—

STAN: These bills, yes?

AMY: Bills?

STAN: Must be very satisfying to burn old bills. To know that nothing's hanging over your head. Here.

> (*He gets a metal wastebasket.*)

This is the safe way to do it.

> (*She hesitates, then tosses the letters into the basket. She picks up the matches, looks at him. He nods. She lights a match and tosses it into the basket. A second passes as the letters burn.*)

The burning of the letters helps underscore Amy's decision to let go of an unhealthy obsession. That Stan catches her in the act of burning what he recognizes as their correspondence and chooses to pretend that she is burning bills suggests an unspoken offer to Amy that he will never confront her openly with his knowledge. His pretense, of course, is another kind of transformation, and her agreement signals that they will collaborate on a fiction to save each other and themselves from embarrassment.

In each of the passages I've cited—the upsetting of the smelling salts, the ripping of the pants, and the burning of the letters—the meaning of the scene is conveyed by disturbing or destroying objects.

Assignment Three: Choose an object and define the relationship between two characters through the way they negotiate over it, adding punctuation to the scene by transforming the object in some way—by modifying it, destroying it, or using it in a manner for which it was not intended.

By *Rhiannon Ross*

(Mother's dining room. Mother is sixty-something and wears a headscarf. Debby, her daughter, is in her thirties. They stand in front of a china cabinet.)

MOTHER: Well, how about the Fiestaware, Deb? You like bright colors.

DEBBY: No, Mother. I want the Oatmeal glass. The dishes you promised me.[1]

MOTHER: I promised Donna the Oatmeal.

DEBBY: How could you have promised her?

MOTHER: I did.

DEBBY: She doesn't even care about things like that . . .

MOTHER: Well, she does now.

DEBBY: . . . or dolls. Or the piano, for that matter.

MOTHER: I'm sorry for giving her the piano. There are still more dolls.

DEBBY: The ones she didn't want?

MOTHER: She always got your hand-me-downs.[2] How about this Depression glass?

(Hands her a plate, which Debby accepts, but doesn't look at.)

DEBBY: I don't want the Depression glass, either. I want the Oatmeal, the ones you promised me.

(Tries to hand plate back, but Mom turns away to search in china cabinet.)

MOTHER: Do you like Carnival glass?

(Takes down a bowl.)

Donna wants it but maybe I can talk her into . . .

DEBBY: Why do you insist on giving me the dishes I don't want?[3]

MOTHER: They're all antiques. What does it matter?

DEBBY: 'Cause I don't like Depression glass . . . or Fiesta.

MOTHER: They're worth money . . .

DEBBY: Do you want us to sell them?

MOTHER: Definitely not! Think of them as keepsakes.

DEBBY: Well, I don't want this one as a keepsake!

(Attempts to return to cabinet, but in her haste, hits china cabinet door instead. Plate breaks on the end.)[4]

MOTHER *(Snapping)*: Be careful!

DEBBY: Oh, Mother! I'm sorry.

MOTHER: Oh, Debraaaaaaaaa!

(Replaces bowl in cabinet.)

DEBBY: Sooooorrrrryyyyy!

(Looks at plate; starts to giggle.)

MOTHER: Just what is so . . .

DEBBY: Well, look at it now.

(Exhibits plate.)

It *is* pretty depressing!

MOTHER: That's not funny!

(Yanks plate from her.)

DEBBY: Oh, Mo THER!

MOTHER: Ouch!

DEBBY: Didya cut yourself?

MOTHER: Yes![5]

DEBBY: Let me see your hand . . .

MOTHER *(Pulling away):* It's fine! It's the plate that's not fine!
  (She begins to suck on the inside of her hand.)

DEBBY: I didn't mean to . . .

MOTHER: You've always been clumsy . . .[6]

DEBBY: I *said* I'm sorry.
  (Softer.)
You're bleeding, Mama . . .
  (Mother takes dishtowel from back of dining chair and wraps hand.)

MOTHER: I said I'm fine! You know, I'd think you'd want some of my dishes.

DEBBY: Well, I don't.

MOTHER: What?
  (She bends down, picks up shard from floor.)

DEBBY: . . . or your dolls or your furniture or your clothes . . .

MOTHER: The piano?

DEBBY: Or the piano . . . well, I did, but . . .

MOTHER *(Rises):* Then what *do* you want, Debra?
  (Blood can be seen on towel.)[7]

DEBBY *(Softly):* Oh, Mother . . .[8]

MOTHER *(Deep sigh):* Alright, alright . . . I'll talk to Donna, maybe she'll be okay with just the Carnival.

1. And we begin to figure things out. We see the mother is wearing a headscarf, which is often a tip-off of chemotherapy for cancer, and we see that she is determining which of her children is going to get what stuff, and we can smell the issue of mortality.

2. Through the negotiation over the objects—the dishes, the piano, the dolls—we can appreciate the competition between Donna and Debby. Mother's line about Donna having gotten Debby's hand-me-downs also nicely establishes who is the elder sister and opens up speculation as to who was likely to have been treated more indulgently given her age.

3. This is a little on the head. In the audience, we've already figured out

Mother is doing this, and it's a little disappointing to be told what we've already figured out. Again, this is an instance in which the unspoken would probably have more power.

4. The accidental breaking of the china gives physical expression to the friction between mother and daughter.

5. The idea of breaking or transforming an object applies to people as well, as we can see with Mother's cut. The discord between them has now led to a physical injury.

6. This is one of those overly evaluative lines I hope you'll try to avoid, a line in which one character sticks a label on another and so short-circuits the opportunity for us in the audience to figure out that the mother thinks of Debby as being clumsy. How could you do this line if "clumsy" had to be an unspoken word?

7. The blood on the towel is very effective, suggesting the seriousness of the cut and underscoring the intimations of mortality that are so much a part of this scene.

8. I'm pleased Debby doesn't respond to Mother's "Then what do you want, Debra?" Unanswered questions onstage can be very potent because, not having the resolution provided by a truthful response, we in the audience instantly start to speculate for ourselves.

Perhaps the master of unanswered questions is Harold Pinter. His play, *The Collection*, is filled with characters asking each other questions which either remain unanswered or are answered with intentionally transparent lies or flippancy laced with hostility. Filing a stage with unanswered questions is like setting up a bunch of little time bombs, which raises the tension considerably. This technique is a large part of Pinter's effectiveness. Of course, this can be overdone, but then any device can be employed to the point of absurdity

In improvisational theatre, some actors believe that questions are generally to be avoided in scenes. If you ask your scene partner, "How did you lose your entire inheritance?" you're putting your partner into a situation in which he or she has sole responsibility to invent a story. Since the point of improvisation is that actors are supposed to be creating together, to manipulate your partner into having to invent on his or her own is considered rude.

Of course, we're not improvising with a partner when we write. But questions in written pieces can be dangerous for other reasons. When one character demands an explanation from another, you the writer run the risk of succumbing to the impulse to have the second character supply that explanation, to tell the truth as he or she sees it. But, as I've said before (and will undoubtedly say again), anything you have a character explain onstage robs the audience the opportunity to participate in coming up with their own theories.

Most of this scene works well, though as in some of my comments on other scenes, I'd be a lot happier and I think the scene would be a little zippier if you were able to cut down on some of the lines in the past tense at the beginning of the scene.

By Bonnie King

(The setting is the area of the emergency department where psychiatric patients are evaluated for admission. On stage are a gray metal desk, a swivel chair with wheels, a wall phone, an intercom, a large metal wastebasket and two gurneys with privacy curtains pulled back. An open door shows a sink and toilet.)

BETH'S VOICE (Over the intercom): Hillie and I are going to that meeting with Figerella and administration to fight for security.[1] If any psych patients come in, the secretary will send them back. Page me and take vital signs.

SANDY (Pushes the button): Okay. I'll hold the fort.

(Sandy sits at the desk reading her latest copy of The American Journal of Psychiatric Nursing. She fishes a Hershey chocolate bar from the pocket of her white lab coat. It's too melted to be neatly eaten, so she lays the magazine on the desk and avidly licks the chocolate off of the silver foil, leaning forward, careful not to let any drop on the lap of her white uniform. When the last bit of chocolate is finished, she drops the sticky silver wrapper into the big metal wastebasket beside the desk and licks what was left of the chocolate off her fingers. She goes into the bathroom, one assumes to wash her hands. Bill, a red-faced, slim, wiry guy in his forties, *staggers into the room, leans on the desk, unzips his jeans and, with his back to the audience, begins to relieve himself into the wastebasket.*[2] *Sandy emerges from the bathroom.)*

SANDY: Hey!

(Bill whirls toward her liberally watering the whole area, her shoes included.)[3]

BILL: Listen, nurse, I'd stop, I just ain't got the brakes.

(He turns back to the wastebasket, reaims, silent until finished, shakes off, and zippers up.)

SANDY: Oh, my goodness.

BILL: You look too young to be a nurse. Oh, those stripes on your arm means you're a student, huh, a nurseling?[4] What's your name, nurseling?

SANDY: Sandy Springer.

BILL: They call me Cowboy Bill. Used to ride the rodeos 'til I broke one too many bones. Moved back to Pittsburgh so's my old lady could be with her family, then the bitch goes and kicks me out.

(He shakes his head and rolls his eyes.)

Ya look too young to be a bitch. I guess I ought to apologize for pissing on your shoes.

SANDY: Yes.

BILL: But totally unlike me.

(Bill leans his elbows on the gurney and peers at her, laughing at his own joke.)

Better mop up this puddle or somebody might slip.

(Sandy goes to leave the room, but Bill blocks her way. Sandy starts to duck around him but Bill pretends to slip and fall against her, herding her against the wall, his face suddenly fiery-eyed and menacing.[5]*)*

You scared?

SANDY: Sure. Sure, I am.

(She starts crying, really sobbing, wide-mouthed and loud. Bill holds his hand over her mouth to muffle the sound.)

BILL: If ya don't give Cowboy Bill any trouble, ya don't have nothin' to worry about. Com' on sweetheart. Lots of ladies would love to get this close to me. Bet you've never had a real man before. Just them little boys with their little dicks.

(His lips smear kisses on her tear-soaked face. His other hand slides up from her waist to her breast.)
You know, for such a tiny bit of a girl you sure got nice big boobs.

(He bends his knees so he can rub himself between her legs. She draws her thighs together, tight.)
Oh, so you are a bitch, after all.

(He pulls a knife from his pocket, flicks it open, and points the knife at her jugular.)
Pull up your skirt and spread those legs or I'll cut your pretty little throat.

(Tommy, a tall muscular man with spiked blond hair and a blond goatee, wearing jeans, a tee shirt, and a leather jacket, enters the room.)

TOMMY: Get away from her.

(Tommy grabs the back of Bill's shirt, picks him up with little effort, and whispers loudly through clenched teeth into the ear of the dangling man.)
Now drop the knife.

(He twists Bill's arm behind his back forcibly until Bill finally drops the knife.)

BILL: Let go. You're choking me.

TOMMY: If I was fucking choking you, you wouldn't be able to fucking talk.

(Tommy carries Bill like a baby and drops Bill into the wastebasket, buttocks first.[6])
That should hold him. Go get Beth. Tell her her favorite patient, Tommy Travers, says she better get her ass back here, pronto. Take that knife with you.

(Sandy picks up the knife and walks out of the room. Tommy sits on the desk and rests his feet on Bill's shoulders, preventing him from getting out of the wastebasket.)

1. Given what happens later in the scene, I think it's a little too neat that the meeting Beth is going to is about security.

2. Bill using the wastebasket as a urinal certainly qualifies as the misuse of an object. It also tips us off that he doesn't respect boundaries much and suggests that he is capable of even more appalling behavior.

3. I can't imagine how this would be staged in a theatre. Now, there are actors who will appear onstage in virtually any stage of undress. And certainly there are those who, in gestures of bravado, will do almost anything. But faking urination when the character turns downstage and theoretically is exposed is a problem (unless of course the actor were actually urinating, which—aside from matters of taste—I think would jar the audience out of their involvement in the action of the play), not to mention that the actor would have to be a pretty expert marksman to make certain that he hit Sandy's shoes.

   Part of what you need to be concerned with when writing a play is the idea of replicable action. That is to say, what you ask to be accomplished onstage every performance must be something that *can* be accomplished every performance.

4. Bill converting the word "nurse" into "nurseling" is his way of converting her to someone with less status and authority. The names we choose for ourselves or use for others convey much about the respect in which we hold the people they represent.

5. This is a negotiation over space, which I will discuss in Lesson 4.

6. Tommy holding Bill in the trash can turns the can into a tool for imprisonment, which is not what it was constructed to do. So now the can has been used both as a urinal and a trap. Of course, the fact that it is a trash can is significant—it suggests that Bill is human trash.

This scene raises the question of how one treats distasteful and offensive behavior onstage. Bill's behavior in this scene is ugly, and the actor playing Bill is called upon to literally do things that are off-putting. I choose to avoid such literal depictions of behavior onstage because I think it they are at odds with the nature of stage action. As I said above, I believe that theatre is built on transformations and metaphor. In my experience, action that is too literal onstage has the paradoxical effect of reminding the audience that the rest of the action, as well as the setting and the other metaphoric elements, aren't real. There will be some in the audience who will be disturbed that an actor is violently groping the breasts of an actress. This will give rise to the thought, "Well, of course, it's rehearsed so the actress has given the actor permission to grope her." This flies against what the audience is supposed to believe—that Bill is terrorizing Sandy. It reminds the audience that what is happening onstage is artifice. I think that the compact between the audience and stage is difficult enough to maintain without pushing matters this far. Personal opinion.

As written, I think this is better suited for the screen. Through editing, sound, and camera placement, one could suggest much of what Bill does without having to show it. Indeed, I think *not* showing is the more powerful choice because—between the sounds of his zipper being unzipped and liquid hitting the inside of the trash can—the audience will have no trouble imagining what he is up to. When Sandy returns, the look on her face and the direction in which she is looking will clinch the impression. This is, again, an example of premises and conclusions in action.

4

LESSON

Other Negotiations

IN CHARLIE CHAPLIN'S FILM THE GREAT DICTATOR, CHAPLIN PLAYS Adenoid Hynkel (a cartoon version of Hitler) and Jack Oakie plays Spumoni (Mussolini). The two loathe each other, but, for political reasons, they have to pretend to get along. Still, they can't help indulging in gambits of one-upsmanship. At one point, Hynkel suggests they go to his private barber shop. The two men sit in barber chairs. Hynkel notices Spumoni's chair is a little higher than his and surreptitiously cranks his own up an inch. Spumoni then cranks his up an inch. Soon, there's no pretense of surreptitiousness—they're both cranking away like crazy until their chairs are virtually pressing them against the ceiling. They are negotiating over height.

I introduced the concept of negotiation with the negotiation over physical objects, but one can negotiate over anything to which value can be attached. As the Chaplin scene establishes, value can indeed be attached to elevation.

Elevation and status are commonly correlated, so the negotiation over height is often a metaphor for a negotiation over status. Certainly Shakespeare knew this. Placing Juliet on a balcony was a way for Shakespeare to make visual Romeo's aspirations. (He would not get the same effect if he had Romeo court her by calling down into a pit.)

Elevation is also commonly linked to virtue. We think of Heaven as being up and the Hell to which Twain consigned his antagonist as being down. Similarly, in his novel *The Time Machine*, H. G. Wells establishes that the gentle, childlike Eloi live on the earth's surface and the monstrous, cannibalistic Morlocks live underground.

One can negotiate over spacial concepts other than elevation. The war over real estate is a constant theme in movies. The battles between cattle barons, farmers, marshals, outlaws, and the railroads over who will call the shots in a town or on the range is the heart of many Westerns, among them *Shane*, *The Magnificent Seven*, *Once upon a Time in the West*, *The Unforgiven*, *My Darling Clementine*, and *The Westerner*. In war films (*The Longest Day*, *Saving Private Ryan*, *Is Paris Burning?*, *The Sands of Iwo Jima*, *Lawrence of Arabia*, etc.), the competing interests doing battle over territory are governments. Likewise, the gangsters of *The Godfather*, *Goodfellas*, *Little Caesar*, and *The Untouchables* go to the mattresses for dominance over turf.

Territorial conflicts are also common onstage. John Guare's *Six Degrees of Separation* is about a young man who assumes an identity to con his way into a social circle beyond his reach. David Henry Hwang's *The Golden Child* concerns the introduction of Christianity into a traditional Chinese merchant's home and the havoc this wreaks on the merchant and his three wives. Margaret, the minor French princess who dominates Shakespeare's *Henry* VI cycle, marries a weak English king and, after her arrival, so destabilizes her husband's court that she triggers a bloody civil war. All of these plays involve the disruptions outsiders make on the equilibria of the worlds into which they plunge.

Single-set plays are particularly prone to concern themselves with this motif. The set tends to represent the home or power base of one character or group of characters. When people from the outside appear and attempt to stay, the dramatic issue is whether the location will fall under the newcomers' sway. Blanche "invades" Stanley's kingdom in A *Streetcar Named Desire*. Felix moves into Oscar's apartment in *The Odd Couple*. In Donald Margulies' *Collected Stories*, a student goes from being an awkward guest in her mentor's house to moving around it as if it were her second home, until, in the last scene, having betrayed her mentor's trust, she is ejected.

You can negotiate over space on a smaller scale than a range, a town, or an apartment, of course. In the next-to-last scene of *Streetcar*, Blanche wants to pass through a room. She asks Stanley to stand back. He tells her she has plenty of room to get by. Of course she doesn't and that's the point. When directors block a play, what they are doing is having the characters negotiate over space in a way that makes the relationships of the characters come alive.

(Incidentally, blocking in film adds another dimension of spacial negotiation, because the characters not only move in relationship to each other, but to the camera, which frequently changes its perspective by jumping from shot to shot within a sequence or shifting its position during the course of a shot. In a play, the playgoers view the action from a constant position—the seats to which they have been assigned. In a film, the director chooses the vantage points from which the action is seen, so the director has a stronger moment-to-moment hand in shaping the audience's experience of the dramatic material.)

You can negotiate over time, too. That's what the term *timing* addresses—the subtle meaning that can be invested in an action or a speech through the way a performer plays with speed, hesitation, momentum, etc. The same text spoken with different timing changes the meaning of the text.

HUSBAND: What do you say we visit my mother?

WIFE (*Instantly*): Let's go.

This means something different than—

HUSBAND: What do you say we visit my mother?

   (*Pause, then—*)

WIFE: Let's go.

The different use of time changes the meaning of the scene. This is one of the reasons that Harold Pinter so carefully scores the beats and pauses in his scripts. He knows that the silences often convey as much about what is going on between his characters as do the words.

I once ran into a friend who was costarring on Broadway in a musical with a leading lady of international reputation. He told me that, having grown up in a chilly climate, the star liked turning down the thermostat of the theatre in which the show was playing. The dancers in the show were not happy; cold muscles are more easily injured—a negotiation over temperature.

One can also negotiate over sound. The motorcycle riders who gun their hogs in the middle of the night in quiet residential districts do it partially for the thrill of waking the bourgeoisie in their beds. Anyone who has either been a teenager with a stereo or been the parent of a teenager with a stereo is familiar with this form of negotiation.

To go back to *The Time Machine*, H. G. Wells establishes that the Morlocks flourish in the dark. Bram Stoker has *Dracula*'s title character flourish when the sun is in retreat. Both Wells and Stoker are here invoking the common correlation between light and dark and good and evil. (Shakespeare is filled with lines equating dark complexions with evil natures. Contemporary audiences have to choose not to take this too seriously in these racially charged times.) Yes, you can negotiate over light.

A clever dramatist can subvert the cliché. In Frederick Knott's *Wait Until Dark*, darkness is the blind heroine's friend. She has an advantage over the sighted villains when the lights are out. The suspenseful climax of the play (and the film derived from it) comes when she cannot close a refrigerator door that beams its tiny light into the room. This small light tips the playing field to her assailant's advantage.

In his farce *Black Comedy*, Peter Shaffer inverts the values by establishing a theatrical convention that light on the stage represents darkness and vice versa. When somebody lights a match, for instance, the stage light in that area dims. The end of the play comes when characters whose schemes will be undone if the lights come on are suddenly plunged into a blackout. (As the lights in reality come on, the stage lights go out.)

So, to summarize—you can negotiate over objects, space, time, light, temperature, sound. What else?

Well, in David Mamet's *American Buffalo*, Teach and Bobby (whether Bobby is entirely aware of it or not), negotiate for the loyalty of Donny, the proprietor of the junk store in which the play is set. In Wendy Wasserstein's *The Heidi Chronicles*, yuppie entrepreneur Scoop and idealistic gay doctor Peter compete for the allegiance of the title character. So evidently you can negotiate over people's favor. In fact, I'd go so far as to say that any script dealing with three characters or more is inevitably going to involve the issue of who is going to side with whom, whether romantically or politically.

One can also negotiate over words, particularly charged words such as proper names.

President Carter chose to be referred to in official literature as "Jimmy Carter" rather than "James E. Carter," consistent with his desire to be perceived as an ordinary citizen who happened to be President. (He also made some of his broadcasts to the American people dressed in a sweater rather than a tie and jacket.)

Director-choreographer Jerome Robbins earned the contempt of many in the 1950s by cooperating with the House Committee on Un-American Activities and naming names, thereby damaging the lives of many associates. Zero Mostel, who had been blacklisted, agreed to work with Robbins on *A Funny Thing Happened on the Way to the Forum* and *Fiddler on the Roof*, but instead of referring to him as "Jerry" or "Mr. Robbins," he called him "Loose Lips." Of course, Robbins himself had changed his name; he was born "Rabinowitz." The switch from "Rabinowitz" to "Robbins" said something about how he wished to be perceived at a time when anti-Semitism was more overt. The switch from "Robbins" to "Loose Lips" says a good deal about how he sometimes actually was perceived.

Characters of low status gain stature in stories when they are given new names. This often comes up in pieces based on the Cinderella model. In Shaw's *Pygmalion*, "Liza" becomes "Miss Doolittle." In Frank Capra's film *Lady for a Day* (based on the Damon Runyon story "Madame La Gimp"), a street beggar named "Apple Annie" is passed off as a society lady named "Mrs. E. Worthington Manville." In their script for the film *One, Two, Three*, Billy Wilder and I. A. L. Diamond turn the Cinderella character into a scruffy East German communist whom a businessman has to pass off as a count, complete with a title purchased from a bankrupt aristocrat. In *Lawrence of Arabia* (directed by David Lean from a screenplay by Robert Bolt and Michael Wilson), the British soldier T. E. Lawrence is given a new name by the Arab guerillas he leads, "El Aurens."

The most extreme transformations of name occur when a character is in disguise. Shakespeare is full of disguises, frequently of women dressed as men. In *Merchant of Venice*, Portia disguises herself as a young male lawyer named Balthasar. In *Twelfth Night*, Viola disguises herself as a boy named Cesario. *As You Like It*'s Rosalind transforms herself into Ganymede. This device may have been attractive to Shakespeare because the women's parts in his productions were played by boys, so these plays allowed a boy playing a woman to pretend to be a boy. (In his film

Victor/Victoria, Blake Edwards switched this by having a woman playing a man pretending to be a woman.)

The reverse has been popular fodder for comedy as well. Brandon Thomas' *Charley's Aunt* is about a student who has to pretend to be a woman to act as a chaperone for himself. Dustin Hoffman and Robin Williams had hits in *Tootsie* and *Mrs. Doubtfire*, getting a little sensitivity training while putting on skirts. In *Some Like It Hot*, Billy Wilder and I. A. L. Diamond put two men (Jack Lemmon and Tony Curtis) into skirts to hide in an all-female band to escape from gangsters in Chicago.

In this light, I am particularly tickled by the setups of two plays by James Sherman, *Beau Jest* and *Jest a Second*. In the first play, a Jewish woman, to please her parents, hires a non-Jewish actor named Kris to pretend to be her Jewish boyfriend, a Dr. Steinberg. (He is mostly able to pull this off because he's acted in *Fiddler on the Roof.*) In the second play, Kris dresses up as a woman so that he can pretend (for the benefit of the same parents) to be the girlfriend his closeted gay brother-in-law thinks he needs.

One can also negotiate over differing values or ideas.

An example of character being revealed through the negotiation over ideas appears in the second scene of my play *With and Without*. The story concerns a married couple named Mark and Shelly and the difficulty they face when they have to cope with Jill, a friend who has good reason to believe that her husband Russ is leaving her. (The four were supposed to share a vacation house for the week, and only Mark, Shelley, and Jill have shown up on schedule.) At this point in the play, Jill has tired of trying to track down her missing husband by telephone and suggests a distraction.

JILL: What we should do, probably, is rent a video. Something awful. Something we can mock. You ever see *Return to Peyton Place*?

MARK: No.

JILL: It was on one of the cable channels. Russ and I watched it. All these incredible archaic nineteen-fifties values topped off with Fifties hair and paperback versions of Freud. So-and-so's shocking secret. The scandal that rocked a town.

MARK: Which was?

JILL: Probably somebody slept with somebody they weren't supposed to. Isn't that what it always is? Actually, it's almost quaint. Looking at what was supposed to be shocking, daring. Kind of a nostalgia rush. Like Jane Russell's boobs in that Western.

MARK: *The Outlaw.*

JILL (*To Shelly*): Trust a man to remember that, hunh?

> (*Mark looks at Shelly pointedly. Jill doesn't notice.*)

Sometimes I think—you know, to go back to a world where Jane Russell's cleavage was shocking. Who could be shocked by that today, right? Hell, you see more boobs today in *Disney* movies. Jessica Rabbit.

MARK: I read someplace that he was an ass man.

JILL: Who?

MARK: Disney. That if you look at a lot of the cartoons, you'll see that there's a lot of fanny patting.

JILL: Are you saying Disney had a secret lust for Minnie Mouse?

MARK: Of course, that's exactly what I'm saying.

JILL: Then what *are* you saying?

MARK: Just thought I'd toss in a little ancillary trivia.

JILL: That Disney was an ass man.

MARK: That's what I read. Or heard.

JILL: What does this have to do with what we were discussing?

MARK: Were we discussing something? Something in particular?

JILL: I thought we were. I was making a point, and I don't usually make points if I'm not discussing something. But then you jump in with that Jane Russell thing—

MARK: I didn't bring up Jane Russell. *You* brought up Jane Russell.

JILL: You brought up Minnie Mouse's ass.

MARK: I brought up Walt Disney.

JILL: Yeah, why did you do that?

MARK: I'm sorry.

JILL: Well, you should be. What does it matter, really, what Walt Disney was? I mean, he's gone, and he's left behind all these wonderful films, so why do you have to attack him?

MARK: Is that what I was doing?

JILL: You called him an ass man.

MARK: You think that was an attack?

JILL: You think that was a compliment?

MARK: I think it's just a comment. With no particular value attached.

JILL: Sometimes I think it would be nice to put up a fence around people and they would be, like, protected people? No matter what you dug up about them, we don't want to know. Like Disney. I don't want to know. Or that stuff about Errol Flynn maybe being a Nazi spy. Or Joan Crawford and the coat hangers. Or whatever Chaplin was supposed to have done. Leave it alone, you know? Leave it alone. What's going to be helped by learning shitty things about people like that? . . . . . Isn't there a point where the good stuff they've done outweighs the smaller shit? . . . . .

MARK: If you're asking me if I think there should be special rules for a certain class of people, no I don't think there should be special rules. I don't think being a celebrity should protect someone from the consequences of behaving badly.

JILL: No, see, this is what you don't get. I'm not talking about *them*. I'm not talking about protecting *them*. I'm talking about protecting *us*.

MARK: What from?

SHELLY: Disillusion.

JILL: See? She gets it. Your wife gets it. Sometimes the heart only can take so much. You don't want more bad news. Especially unnecessary bad news. Stuff that you can't change. I can't change that Errol Flynn was a Nazi spy, if he was. But knowing that changes me. It makes me not be able to enjoy *Robin Hood*. And I'd rather enjoy *Robin Hood* than know something I can't change.

MARK: You'd rather not know.

JILL: I'd rather not know.

MARK: So why have you been on the phone the past hour and a half?

In this passage, the subject of what we do or do not know about celebrities' morals is not significant in itself. It is supposed to be a trivial, safe topic for the three of them to bat about. What the discussion over Minnie Mouse and Errol Flynn reveals is not vital information about the cartoon character and the movie star but the politics of the relationship between Jill, Mark, and Shelly, particularly the pleasure Jill gets out of teasing Mark and the fact that Mark doesn't get as much pleasure as she imagines out of being teased. Also the line, "Trust a man to remember that, hunh?," is meant to reaffirm the idea that much of the play is rooted in the conflict between the genders' perspectives and that Jill isn't above trivializing the issues in pursuit of advantage. Shelly says less than the others in this scene, which has the consequence of lending more weight to what she does say. When she comments, "Disillusion," she demonstrates her ability to put into one word the essence of Jill's argument and also implies the empathy she feels for her friend. Though she has fewer lines, Shelly ends up registering as the wisest person in the scene.

> **Assignment Four:** I want another negotiation, but this time, instead of centering around an object, I want you to define characters' relationship to each other primarily through some other kind of negotiation.

By *Patsy Souza*

(*Two women—Lila (age 32) and Athari (age 19)—sit at a table outside a Starbucks on Kuwait's sea front. Both women are dressed in* abayas, *traditional Arabian garments. Lila's abaya is pulled taut over her hair, only her face showing. Athari's rests loosely on her shoulders, hair uncovered.*)[1]

LILA: Cover your head, you're asking for trouble. Anyone could pass by.[2]

ATHARI: Relax! And who cares . . . this is 1999, not 1939. Things change.

LILA: Things change in New York City, maybe London. Little changes in Kuwait City. Why did you want to stop here anyway?[3]

(*Lila glances at her watch.*)

It's almost time for prayer, we should be home.[4]

ATHARI: I'm meeting someone.

(*Athari looks around.*)

LILA: Who?

(*Athari waves, a Filipino woman approaches, sets a plastic shopping bag on the table. Athari passes a fist full of Kuwaiti dinars to her, the woman walks away. Lila follows the transaction with her eyes and then stares at Athari.*)
Tell me that's not what I think it is.[5]

ATHARI: Okay . . . it's not two pounds of hickory smoked bacon, it's not a Black Forest ham.

(*She removes the bag from the table and settles it at her feet. Visibly shaken, Lila pulls her abaya tighter around her face and hisses at Athari.*)

LILA: Are you insane? If Father even thought you ate pork, let alone bought it on the black market, he would never let you leave Kuwait again.[6] And where do you plan on cooking it?

ATHARI: Cook will fix it.[7] Anyway, you think they will stone me because I have acquired a taste for BLTs?

LILA: Marriage. Only marriage is going to get you under control.[8] It was a mistake letting you go away to school. Leave the bag and let's go.

(*Lila puts money on the table, gathers up her car keys and puts on her designer sunglasses in preparation to leave. Athari shrugs, her abaya falling off one shoulder. She leans down and retrieves the bag.[9]*)

ATHARI: I need to stop for tomatoes.

1. It is instantly arresting to juxtapose a Starbucks with women in abayas. This also quickly suggests something of what the scene turns out to be about—the collision of the traditional customs of Arab women to which Lila adheres and the Western culture to which Athari has been exposed and by which she has been "corrupted."

2. Lila urging Athari to cover herself with the abaya because "anyone" might see her swiftly suggests both Lila's conservative nature and Athari's more liberated one. This also tells us a good deal about the society.

3. This reference to Kuwait City comes across as the author seizing on a

device to inform the audience of the scene's location. Both Lila and Athari know they are in Kuwait City, so Lila wouldn't need to inform Athari of it.

4. This detail, suggesting that a normal part of their lives is to be home at a specific time for prayer, goes a long way toward conveying where they are. At this point, I might not have figured the specific location mentioned in the stage directions, but, between what they're wearing, the likely presence of Arabic lettering somewhere on the store's signs, and this detail about scheduled prayer, I would certainly have an idea of what part of the world you're dealing with.

5. The introduction of a mysterious object through a mysterious transaction!

6. I think you don't have to be quite this obvious. For one thing, we in the audience have already figured out that we've witnessed a black market transaction, so to label it such isn't necessary. Also, we know that bacon and ham are pork and a general audience is probably aware of the religious prohibitions against pork. You could easily have gotten your point across with, "If Father knew what that is, let alone how you got it, he would never let you leave Kuwait again." Incidentally, this Kuwait reference seems to me to be less forced than the earlier one was. Also the "again" suggests that Athari has indeed been out of the country and probably picked up her dangerous tastes there.

7. "Cook will fix it," suggests (a) that this is a family wealthy enough to have a cook on staff, and (b) that cook is already accustomed to doing things that aren't strictly according to the rules. This further implies that it is not uncommon for people with money in Kuwait to wink a little at formal strictures.

8. The way Lila brings up marriage offers further insight into the traditional role of women in Kuwait society.

9. Lila's car keys and her designer sunglasses give strong hints as to the degree she herself has been Westernized. That Athari doesn't much care if her abaya falls off one shoulder and, despite her sister's urg-

ing, her insistence on taking the bag, are two actions that give expression to Athari's rebelliousness.

Except for the couple of points where I think you're being a little overt in conveying information, this is done adroitly. Through the use of the objects, you not only manage to convey the politics between the two sisters but also something of the role of women under the customs and laws of Kuwait. The line, "you think they will stone me because I have acquired a taste for BLTs?" is chilling because we've heard of instances of women being stoned for "transgressions" of a not much more serious nature.

By *Michael Johnson-Chase*

(*Ordinary-looking kitchen in a suburban house outside a large city somewhere in America. Sondra sits at the kitchen table, eating a bowl of cereal. Teresa enters, hesitates, begins cleaning off a table messy with dishes.*)

TERESA: Captain Crunch?

SONDRA: Yea.

TERESA: Can't believe I bought that crap.[1] Wreck your teeth.

SONDRA: Don't care about my teeth. My teeth are ugly.

TERESA: You seen Adele?

SONDRA: She had breakfast before.[2]

TERESA: I'm tired of cleaning up after her.

(*Sondra takes her dish to the sink.*)

SONDRA: Can I get my ears pierced?

TERESA: You're too young, Sondra.

SONDRA: Come on. Adele's got a nose ring.

TERESA: She's twenty-eight.

SONDRA: Yea, sure. And going on eight.

TERESA: Watch your mouth.

SONDRA: She has another ring.

TERESA: Where—

SONDRA: Why can't I get my ears pierced? I've already got the posts.[3]

TERESA: No, Sondra! Stop asking me.

    (She sees the remains of something in the garbage.)

What's this?

SONDRA: What?

TERESA: This food.

SONDRA: Something Adele ate.

TERESA: What was it?

SONDRA: Beats me. Looked like cow shit.

TERESA *(Yelling offstage)*: Adele. . . . Adele!

ADELE *(From offstage)*: What?

TERESA: Come here.

ADELE: Why?

TERESA: Got something to ask you.

ADELE: What?

TERESA: Just come here.[4]

    (Pause. Adele enters in a wheelchair, sporting a nose ring.)[5]

ADELE: What?

TERESA: What did you have for breakfast?

ADELE: A muffin.

TERESA: What kind of muffin?

ADELE: I don't know. One of those kinds you bought.

TERESA: One of which kinds I bought?

ADELE: I don't know. What kind did you buy?

TERESA: You don't know?

ADELE: I ate it, that's all. Coulda been blueberry, coulda been strawberry.

TERESA: Bran.

ADELE: OK. Bran.

TERESA: There's a big difference between blueberry or strawberry and bran. In fact, there's a big difference between blueberry and strawberry.[6]

ADELE: There is?

TERESA: Adele.

ADELE: I didn't pay attention, OK?

TERESA: You're not intellectually disabled.

ADELE: Can I go back to my chat room?

TERESA: Not till I find out what you really had for breakfast.

ADELE: Christ.

(*Adele attempts to leave. Teresa blocks her way.*)

TERESA: I'm supposed to be taking care of you. Just tell me what you had and how you got it.

(*Teresa pulls Adele's hair.*)[7]

ADELE: I had a scone.

TERESA: A scone.

ADELE: Yea. With raisins. I cut it in half, toasted the top, and put butter and grape jam on it. It was excellent.

TERESA: Is that really what it was?

ADELE: Well, let's see if I can remember. Since I'm not a retard I oughta be able to figure this out.

TERESA: Adele—

ADELE: Yes, it was a scone, I'm sure of it. But I'm wrong about the raisins. They weren't raisins, they were currants. You know, those little transparent yellow—

TERESA: How did you get it?

ADELE: Why, I think a little bird brought it to me.

TERESA: How did you get it, Adele?

ADELE: Mail order.

(*Teresa applies greater force.*)

TERESA: HOW DID YOU GET IT!

(*Pause.*)

ADELE: You'll never figure it out.

TERESA: So help me, if you've been out of this house without me—

ADELE: How can I go out?

TERESA: Has someone been here? Sondra, has someone been here?

SONDRA: How would I know?

TERESA: You're here, Sondra. You would see them.

SONDRA: I haven't seen anybody.

(Teresa spins Adele's wheelchair dangerously close to the wall.)

TERESA: Someone could have come while I was out shopping for food. Or on Saturdays when Mom comes.[8]

SONDRA: Nobody comes to see Adele.

ADELE: Sure they do. They come when you and Mom are out at the same time. Patty comes over from Trenton sometimes.

TERESA: Nice try.

ADELE: Why not?

TERESA: Patty's on dialysis. . . . So where did you get that scone?

ADELE: From Bob.

TERESA: Sure. He's strapped to a hospital bed and shits his pants all the time.[9]

(Teresa runs the wheelchair along a wall, scraping Adele's arm.)

ADELE: Ouch.

TERESA: What about one of your chat room friends?

ADELE: Patty and Bob are my chat room friends.

TERESA: What about the others?

ADELE: There aren't any others. Nobody else will talk pornography with a paraplegic.

(Teresa abruptly stops the wheelchair.)

TERESA: Where'd the scone come from, Adele?

(Pause.)

ADELE: Give up?

TERESA: Fine. Sure. . . . Yea.

ADELE: It feels so good to have secrets.[10]

TERESA: Adele, this is not OK with me. What would Mom think if she knew I was losing control?[11]

ADELE: Over a scone?

(Teresa kicks Adele's wheelchair.)

TERESA: I'm gonna figure this out. It better not have anything to do with you going outside.

(Pause.)

ADELE: How would I get back in?

TERESA: With a key.

ADELE: Where would I hide a key?

TERESA: Nobody out there can help you, Adele.

(Teresa kicks Adele's wheelchair harder, smashing her knees against the wall.)

You have a seizure, you're dead.[12]

ADELE: I don't care.

TERESA: OK. Fine. You win. . . . So, Sondra, what were you telling me about Adele's ring?

SONDRA: What about it?

TERESA: You want to pierce your ears?

SONDRA: Yea.

TERESA: So what were you saying about Adele's ring?

SONDRA: I said. Well. I said if she has a nose ring I ought to be able to have my ears pierced.

TERESA: You said she had another ring.

SONDRA: No, I—

TERESA: Do you want to get your ears pierced or not?

SONDRA: Yea.

TERESA: Then tell me where the other ring is. Her nipple?

SONDRA: Teresa, you can't—

ADELE: You're crazy.

TERESA: Your vagina?

ADELE: You're really crazy.

SONDRA: Stop it! It's not—

TERESA: Don't tell me! I think I know—

SONDRA: Leave her alone, Teresa! Let her go back to her room.

TERESA: Shut up, Sondra!

(Teresa drops Adele's wheelchair over on its back.)[13]

Gonna have to show me now.

SONDRA: Leave her alone!

TERESA: FUCK OFF!

(Teresa knocks Sondra down, and rifles Adele's blouse.)

Your belly button. . . . That was easy. Your goddamn belly button.

ADELE: No! Don't!

TERESA: I oughta tear it off.

ADELE: No!

TERESA: Stop whining. I'll be careful.

(Pause.)

Clever, Adele. But not clever enough.

(Teresa holds up a key. Pause.)[14]

SONDRA: Can I still get my ears pierced?

TERESA: No.

This is an impressive piece. You dramatize the weird politics of these sisters and the household in a very active manner yet without many direct statements. The exposition is nicely implied. We don't know exactly how Teresa ended up being the head of the family, but I buy that she is and that she can rule over Sondra and Adele. You also excite very complicated feelings about Teresa—on the one hand, she seems to be keeping them alive and afloat; on the other, she is hard-edged and autocratic to the point of violence. Some specifics:

1. I'm not a big fan of lines that begin, "I can't believe—"; they usually are there to sneak in exposition. In my opinion, you'd do better with, "I'm gonna stop buying that crap." This suggests a decision that could be made as well as conveys what you want to establish—that she bought this crap and probably is responsible for buying the groceries in this household. Which further suggests that she is in charge of some of the homemaking duties.

2. That Teresa elicits this kind of answer from Sondra reinforces the impression of Teresa running the household. Of course, at this point we don't know that they're sisters.

3. I very much like the negotiation over the proposed piercing. In an upcoming chapter, I will talk about something I call the Robin Hood effect. This is a good example of that—of establishing given or past circumstances of characters through negotiating over plans. But, as I say, more on this later.

4. Negotiation over space. The fact that Teresa can command Adele to come to her and, later, successfully keep her from leaving reinforces her dominance here.

5. This is a wake-up. For one thing, we're not expecting Adele to be in a chair. For another, we don't usually associate people in chairs with people who wear nose rings.

6. This stimulates curiosity and speculation. Why would Teresa make such a big deal about muffins and their kinds? This is the first hint that perhaps Teresa's concern is with Adele's diet, and Adele's lackadaisical attitude about what she eats may be a reflection of her self-destructive side.

7. An able-bodied person physically abusing someone in a wheelchair is a vivid violation of our sense of the way people are supposed to behave.

8. The first concrete clue as to their relationship. Till this point, it might have been possible to believe that Teresa is Adele and Sondra's mother. Teresa's reference to "Mom" suggests that she is indeed their sister and is occupying a mother's place in their lives.

9. The references to Patty and Bob imply that Adele has a sense of community with others with similar problems. These clues and the argument over the scone lead me to think that she is suffering from diabetes.

10. As I've said before, I generally don't much care for lines in which people overtly describe how they feel about something. I prefer action or lines that give the audience the opportunity to figure out how a character feels.

11. This reference to Mom suggests that the three of them are sharing

this house with the approval of or through an arrangement with their mother, and that Teresa feels answerable to her.

12. Although this doesn't lessen the viewer's dismay at the violence Teresa is visiting upon Adele, the line suggests that her anger is based in a fear the Adele's behavior will threaten her life and the frustration she's feeling about not being able to monitor the situation well enough.

13. Yipes! Just reading this stage direction makes me gasp.

14. A transformation of an object—the decorative pierced navel now is revealed to be a sneaky key ring. A nicely theatrical surprise.

SIDEBAR 2

Themes

ACCORDING TO RECIPE, IF YOU TAKE A PIECE OF MOISTENED STRING, roll it in sugar so that the string is coated, and then dunk it into a container filled with a heated solution made up of sugar and water, crystals will accrete around the string. When you pull the string out of the solution and let it cool, you've got rock candy.

I think of my process of writing plays similarly. I start off with a premise or a character—something analogous to the string. Exploring this premise is akin to dipping the string into what is bubbling in my mind—both conscious and un- —and elements from that soup can't help but crystallize around it. The result: a script that not only addresses the story I set out to tell, but inevitably includes other values and undercurrents I hadn't anticipated.

My play *Porch* started when a friend told me she was going over the books of the family business with her ailing father. If he didn't survive an upcoming operation, he didn't want to leave her without the tools to deal with his estate. The play I wrote certainly builds on that premise, but it also ended up being informed by the experience of a number of women I knew who came to the city from small-town backgrounds, determined to lead progressive, modern, liberated lives, and found that they couldn't entirely deny the gravitational pull of the traditional values from which they fled.

Flyovers began with a story another friend told me of a twenty-fifth high school reunion he attended that turned violent. With his permission, I set out to dramatize his tale. The play that resulted ended up exploring not only the personal dynamic between him and the bully who targeted him, but also the resentment a large chunk of the American public have toward New York, Los Angeles, and Washington, D.C., and the degree to which the people who fly between these three cities impose their taste and will on the rest of the country. In other words, on a personal level I found myself dealing with an antagonist who was a bully. On a social level, I found that this bully had some grounds to view himself as part of a class of people who themselves feel bullied by America's power elite.

As I say, the catalysts for these plays were in experiences related to me by people I knew. Themes accreted to the plays because these concerns were obviously stewing inside me as I was writing.

Edward Albee confirmed that I am not the only one who works this way. In a visit with the playwriting students at the Actors Studio's M.F.A. program, he said that shortly after his play *The Zoo Story* opened off-Broadway he got a letter from a nun who was sure it was a Christian parable. Albee began reading her letter in a bemused mood. But bemusement gave way to realization. Everything she saw in the play was there: all the parallels to scripture, all the symbolism. No, he hadn't sat down intending to write a play that dealt in religious imagery, but he had to acknowledge the hold that these images and ideas had on his imagination and that had been manifested in his work without conscious intention.

Albee said further that he never writes thinking about what a work is supposed to mean. He writes because the characters living in his imagination must claim their space on pages in front of him. He trusts that meaning will arise as he reports what they do and say, but he finds it better not to impose it.

I bet that Shakespeare worked similarly. Logic suggests that a guy who wrote two five-act plays a year by hand, as well as producing, acting, tending to various business ventures, and (according to legend) cutting a broad path through the local taverns, didn't have the *time* to be all that self-conscious about his work. Many of the levels of meaning that the scholars and critics see in Shakespeare's work can't have been consciously intended. I doubt that he picked up his quill saying, "Gee, I'm in the mood to write a cycle of plays about what constitutes legitimate authority." Rather, I believe it occurred to him that some of the stories about kings past might sell a few tickets. That he found issues to engage inherent in the stories he was exploring—issues that were relevant to a society headed by Queen Elizabeth—cannot be disputed, but I believe that exploring these issues was incidental to his writing the plays. Exploring these issues was not the conscious reason he undertook their composition. He didn't start with a thematic concern and then look for a king who would embody that concern.

Which is not to say that the thematic concerns that critics and scholars see in his plays aren't there. For instance, Shakespeare lived long before Sigmund Freud, so he obviously couldn't have meant for the characters of Henry IV, Falstaff, and Hal to represent the dynamic of superego, the id, and the ego. Still, anyone with a grasp of elemental Freudian theory will see this pattern in *Henry IV, Parts 1 and 2* and *Henry V*. The fact that Shakespeare couldn't have intended his plays to dramatize Freudian theory doesn't mean that they don't.

The point is, just because a play may *mean* something, it doesn't follow that the play's genesis was in the desire to convey that meaning. Theme doesn't have to come first. In fact, notwithstanding Lajos Egri's *The Art of Dramatic Writing*, I think theme *rarely* comes first. And I think that's all to the best.

This is not to say that no plays have been undertaken by a writer starting with a theme. There is a fair amount of evidence that at least some of Shaw's and Brecht's works originated with the desire to dramatize ideological points. Still, generally, to begin this way strikes me as being comparable to trying to build a skyscraper from the top down.

One of the perils of starting with theme is that you tend to conceive characters as instruments to illustrate your ideas. The figures who people the stage don't exist for their own sake, but for the purpose of articulating or demonstrating the validity of your insights. This means the characters are more likely to *represent* something than to convey the impression of being human beings full of the warring impulses and internal contradictions that inhabit all human souls.

The most successfully written characters are those who seem to live independent of their authors. When you encounter these characters, you aren't constantly aware of the presence of an Oz-like figure behind the curtain pushing buttons, flipping levers, and sending up smoke. These characters appear to be making their own decisions, prompted to act out of their own concerns and compulsions without any regard to proving an author's thesis.

Yes, Blanche can be viewed as representing the outmoded values of the Old South and Stanley as the cruder, brutal industrial consciousness that, because of historical inevitability, must overwhelm those values, but both exist primarily as people, alive and vital. I doubt if *Streetcar* began with Tennessee Williams deciding to write a symbolic work about a civil war in the soul of postwar America. That he had favorite themes is something that is obvious to anyone familiar with his work, but what continues to attract actors to his plays are the rich challenges of the parts he created, not the appeal of the ideas they represent.

You don't have to *think* about incorporating your thematic concerns into your play. If you are writing truthfully and your characters are behaving in a way that corresponds to reality as you see it, these concerns—your themes—will emerge as the natural consequence of telling your story. When I begin work on a script, I trust that the reason I'm attracted to these characters in this situation is that something about them resonates with something inside me. But I don't look too closely at what that meaning is. I don't want to know too early. I want to discover this as I'm writing. If I don't allow myself to get ahead of me, then there's a pretty fair chance that the audience won't get ahead of me. If I discover what a piece is about during its composition, perhaps the audience will have a parallel process of discovery in the theatre.

I find that developing writers do best when they start out with a character who is alive for them and then explore that character in situations that challenge that character's core beliefs. Usually, by following the behavior that's dictated by the logic of that character's philosophy, a thematic consistency will emerge organically and unforced.

It could be that you had an Aunt Ida who took in every orphan she encountered and eventually scandalized the town by marrying one of them. Now, you may not know what Aunt Ida "means," but you might well be so intrigued by Aunt Ida that you want to write about her. By writing about her, about a third of the way through, you may well discover that the story is about the transformational powers of family. But you have extrapolated that *from* Aunt Ida's story. You didn't start by saying, "Oh, I want to write about the transformational powers of family" and then seize on her as a likely vehicle for that idea. Rather, you have realized that this theme is *within* Aunt Ida's story; you may subsequently realize that the reason you were attracted to her story is that theme was lurking. You start with a desire to explore a character and, through the process of exploring, realize what the thematic underpinnings are.

Different writers find the strings for their rock candy in different places.

I understand that Jules Feiffer has begun some of his scripts simply by starting to write dialogue and then figuring out which characters would say these things to each other under what circumstances and why.

Other writers start with an image. *Sunday in the Park with George* began with James Lapine and Stephen Sondheim speculating on the characters of the figures in Seurat's painting and what kind of person would paint such a huge, emotionally detached painting in which nobody looks at anyone else.

Others may extrapolate from events they've observed or in which they participated, or find characters suggested in a piece of music, or imagine who would live in such a building, or wonder what's going on in the mind of the blurry figure in the corner of a news photo.

What all of these points of origin have in common is that they are specifics that act as catalysts for reactions or speculations by writers— reactions and speculations that are also specifics.

Themes aren't specifics. By their very nature, they tend to be abstractions, abstracted *from* what already exists. While it is easy to extrapolate an abstraction from a specific, the reverse is liable to be frustrating.

I'm not saying a script shouldn't have a sense of purpose or that you shouldn't ultimately know why you are writing the play. But, as Lanford Wilson once said to me (quoting a source he could not recall), "The first draft is written by the artist, the second by the critic." That feels about right.

5

LESSON

Professional Versus Personal

TREVA SILVERMAN AND I ONCE WORKED TOGETHER ON AN IDEA FOR a comedy series. I could not have been luckier in a collaborator; Treva wrote many episodes of *The Mary Tyler Moore Show* (Rhoda was her specialty). As I was new to the world of sitcom creation, Treva took it upon herself to show me the ropes. At one point, she observed that in the traditional sitcom setup, you know automatically what two of your permanent sets will be: the leading character's workplace and that character's home.

And yes, the two places visited most often on *Mary* were the newsroom in which Mary worked and her apartment. And the two places visited most often on *The Bob Newhart Show* and *Murphy Brown*, again, were the leads' offices and residences. And *Taxi* and *Cheers* alternated between scenes in the ensembles' shared workplace and the rooms to where they returned at the ends of their shifts.

This suggests that the central issue in traditional sitcom is the clash between the life at work and the life at home. As I mentioned in *The Dramatist's Toolkit*, George Bernard Shaw (that famous sitcom fan) once wrote that the central drama in a person's life often arises from the conflict between one's professional and personal Imperatives.

This idea doesn't apply only to sitcoms, of course. Most hour-long TV series are set in professional environments, and many of their stories concern the conflicts arising between the characters' professional identities and their personal values. The doctors on the medical series *Chicago Hope* have an obligation to do their best for their patients, but, time and again, this obligation runs up against their revulsion for some of the people under their care. In one story, the gang member who murdered the hospital's lawyer finds himself in the emergency room being treated for a bullet wound by doctors who are also the lawyer's grieving friends; despite their Hippocratic oaths, the doctors understandably aren't deeply motivated to alleviate the killer's pain. In another episode, a surgeon suffers pangs of conscience when he is called on to save the life of a Mafia killer.

Similarly, the officers in Steven Bochco's various cop shows are constantly torn between what the rules say they should do and what their personal sense of justice dictates. *Homicide: A Life on the Streets*, too, is very much about the struggle between the detectives' duties and their domestic problems. *Picket Fences'* two leads are a married couple who also happen to be the town's sheriff and leading physician; the stories often focus on the way in which their jobs put them into professional conflict, which in turn creates discord in their domestic lives.

Though I've referred mostly to television programs so far, the struggle between the professional and the personal is the central dynamic of many plays and films as well. Here's what I wrote in my article for *The Best Plays of 1995–1996* about a play by Nicholas Wright:

"Set in 1934 London, Nicholas Wright's *Mrs. Klein* concerns the psychologist Melanie Klein, her daughter Melitta, and Klein's new assistant, Paula Heimann. The play begins in the wake of Mrs. Klein receiving the news that her only son Hans has died under mysterious circumstances in Hungary. The exploration of those circumstances and the responsibility for them provide much of the humor of the evening.

"Yes, I said humor. I seem to be in the minority, but I think the play is a comedy. A comedy rooted in pain, yes, but a comedy nevertheless. Indeed, there are times it verges on farce. Except, instead of people abruptly slamming in and out of doors at breakneck speed, the three characters abruptly slam in and out of roles. Mrs. Klein is simultaneously a leading light in London's psychoanalytic establishment, a stern employer, and a grieving mother. Melitta is simultaneously her mother's daughter, a grieving sister, and an analyst owing allegiance to a different branch of theory than that of her mother. Paula is simultaneously an employee, a potential surrogate daughter, and (yes) an analyst, too. These three spend the evening shifting their various roles—sometimes locking into analytic poses to dissect each other, sometimes invoking their personal roles to manipulate each other.

"The transitions between roles are often so swift as to induce whiplash. In a key passage late in the play, for instance, Paula leads Mrs. Klein through a line of enquiry that reveals what is likely the truth about Hans's death, triggering a wrenching outburst of emotion from her employer. Barely a minute later, the two trade places and Paula is on the couch being analyzed by Klein. That they can swap status as blithely as changing hats and not, for all their intelligence, recognize this strikes me as wonderfully, subtly funny."

As I wrote, the play is based on the conflict between Mrs. Klein as analyst and Mrs. Klein as mother. Wright's script moves to the point at which Klein clearly chooses to place her professional relationship with her assistant above her relationship with Melitta.

My play *American Enterprise* features a key passage based on this dynamic.

Just outside of Chicago, a nineteenth-century robber baron named George Pullman has built a town he's modestly dubbed Pullman. Part of the town is the factory works where the railroad cars bearing his name are constructed. The other part is the residential area where many employees live, paying him rent. A determinist, Pullman has built the place on the theory that, if his workers live in a properly controlled environment, this environment will shape their characters. In short, the town is designed as a machine to build his idea of perfect citizens.

One employee living in the town, a young man named John Patrick Hopkins, catches Pullman's eye. Hopkins is intelligent, sober, personable, and industrious. Pullman promotes Hopkins from a menial job in the lumberyard to paymaster of the company, a position of prominence.

Hopkins is grateful for Pullman's support, but he has objections to the idea of a town being run as a virtual fiefdom by one man. When Pullman pressures Catholic authorities to reassign a priest with whom Pullman disagrees, Hopkins decides to throw his support to a movement calling for the incorporation of the town of Pullman into the city of Chicago. Pullman calls Hopkins on the carpet.

PULLMAN: Somebody has been forging your name.

HOPKINS: Forging?

PULLMAN (*Showing him petition*): It's a very good forgery. If I didn't know you better, I'd say that this was your signature.

HOPKINS: How did you get this?

PULLMAN: It's in my interests to know who is doing what here.

HOPKINS: It's not a conspiracy, it's a petition.

PULLMAN: It's a call for the destruction of this town.

HOPKINS: It's a call to annex the town into the City of Chicago. To incorporate it.

PULLMAN: Which would lead to its destruction. The point of founding this place was to be removed from Chicago and its corruption. Why should we embrace what I have taken pains to shield us from? Now, we'll run an article in the town paper to the effect that your name has been forged on this thing. I have the editor waiting in the next room.

(*He rises to get the editor.*)

HOPKINS: Don't.

PULLMAN: The sooner we can disassociate you from these—these Democrats, the better.

HOPKINS: I don't choose to be disassociated. I am a Democrat.

PULLMAN: You never told me.

HOPKINS: With all due respect, sir, it was none of your business.

PULLMAN: This company is my business, and I won't have you working against its interests.

HOPKINS: I don't think that I am.

PULLMAN: I don't care what you think.

HOPKINS (*Quietly*): I know. That's one of the reasons I signed the petition.

(*A beat.*)

PULLMAN (*Awkwardly*): Perhaps I did not make myself clear.

HOPKINS: In what way?

PULLMAN: Pat, everybody has a public side and a private side.

HOPKINS: All right.

PULLMAN: Now, your private side has nothing to do with me. Think what you want to think, believe what you want to—vote Democrat if you feel you must. But you're a member of management, you represent the company. You're a public figure. You're a public figure because I chose to *make* you one. By hiring you, promoting you.

HOPKINS (*Quietly*): Have you been unhappy with my work?

PULLMAN: Of course not.

HOPKINS: I've been a competent paymaster?

PULLMAN: There's more to holding down a position than just doing the work.

HOPKINS: I see, it's not enough for me to hold my position, I must also hold yours.

PULLMAN: To not publicly express opinions which conflict with company policy.

HOPKINS: Sir, I am very mindful of all that you have done for me. I'm very grateful.

PULLMAN (*Interrupting*): Which is why you signed that petition.

HOPKINS: The two are not connected.

PULLMAN: Don't you have any idea of the plans I have for you?

(*Hopkins looks at Pullman, not understanding what he's getting at. Pullman proceeds rather stiffly.*)

I'm in my sixties. In good health, thank God, but someday somebody else will have to run this company. My son has demonstrated no particular aptitude, so it's logical I should look for somebody who does. This is what you put at risk.

HOPKINS: And what do you require of me? A promise I'd never do anything you wouldn't?

PULLMAN: Assurances that the company would hold to the principles on which it was founded.

HOPKINS: And if I don't subscribe to those principles?

PULLMAN (*Flaring*): You damn well should. They're what put you where you are. Who were you? What were you? A young man with little education, no money, and no prospects. You started here in the lumberyard, and now look at you. This system has worked for you. It is a gesture of the purest perversity to try to dismantle it.

HOPKINS: I don't see it that way.

PULLMAN (*A plea*): Haven't you got the sense to bend?

HOPKINS: Mr. Pullman, you are a man of principle. It is one of the reasons why people respect you. Why I respect you. What you have built you have built without compromising your principles.

PULLMAN: Yes, well?

HOPKINS: How much respect would you have for me if I were to compromise mine?

PULLMAN (A *beat, then*—): Please clean out your desk before the end of the day.

As you probably noticed, Pullman articulates the dynamic I'm discussing when he says, "Pat, everybody has a public side and a private side." The irony intended is that in this scene it is Pullman himself who is being torn by his public and private sides, or, to translate into the terms I used above, the professional and personal imperatives. On a personal level, Pullman views Hopkins as the son he wishes he had. On the professional, he sees Hopkins as a threat, a man associated with forces looking to dismantle the social machinery of Pullman's town. Ultimately, because Hopkins refuses to compromise, Pullman must jettison the personal role (the surrogate father) in favor of the other (the corporate leader).

The point of the public/private dichotomy is to set up a conflict, which must lead the character to making a choice between the two. In my scene, though Pullman has strong paternal feelings for Hopkins, ultimately he decides to let his role as a corporate leader who must maintain authority overwhelm the side of him that wishes to maintain the relationship with Hopkins. This scene marks the end of their friendship. From this point on in the script, they meet as adversaries.

> **Assignment Five:** Write a scene in which a character's profession puts him or her at odds with personal objectives or values.

By Karyn Lynn Dale

   (A hospital room. A nurse, Beverly, attends an elderly patient named Virginia, who is lying in bed. Virginia's granddaughter, Lynn, is present.)

LYNN: Ask her.

BEVERLY: I can't.

LYNN: Just ask her, please.[1]

BEVERLY: Virginia, do you want to have the biopsy?

(*Virginia, confused, shrugs.*)

LYNN: See?

BEVERLY: Virginia, the doctor told you that you need a biopsy, right? He was here, remember?

VIRGINIA (*Softly*): Yes.

BEVERLY: You signed a paper, Virginia, yes?

VIRGINIA: Yes?

BEVERLY: She remembers.[2]

LYNN: What does she—? Ask if she wants the biopsy.

BEVERLY: Virginia, do you want the biopsy?

VIRGINIA: I . . . don't . . . know . . .

LYNN: Grandma, did you understand what the doctor was saying?

VIRGINIA: I don't know.

BEVERLY (*In a sugar-sweet voice*): Virginia, you know that we care about you at this hospital, right? And we want to help you. You want us to help you feel better, right? You want the biopsy, right?[3]

(*Beverly nods her head. Virginia nods her head automatically in response. Beverly turns to Lynn.*)

See, she said yes.

(*Lynn takes Beverly aside.*)

LYNN: She would say yes to anything right now.[4] She is high on Demerol. She'd buy a piece of the Brooklyn Bridge from you right now, if you asked her nicely. Watch—

(*Moves back to Virginia and speaks sweetly to her, nodding.*)

Purple elephants are dancing on my head, Grandma, right?[5]

(*Virginia nods. Lynn turns to Beverly.*)

Don't you see? She's confused.[6] How can she sign anything on her own?

BEVERLY: The doctor has two psychiatric evaluations that say—

LYNN: "She's capable of making healthcare decisions on her own." I know what the doctor says. But, Beverly—

BEVERLY: I can't evaluate. I'm not a—

LYNN: For God's sake. You don't have to be a psychiatrist to document that she's confused.[7]

BEVERLY: She signed the consent.

LYNN: When she was confused.[8]

BEVERLY: I can't say that.

LYNN: Why not? It's the truth.

BEVERLY: She said she wants—

LYNN: I'll ask her what she wants. Grandma, do you want the doctor to put a telescope down your throat? Do you want the doctor to cut a piece of the mass in your lung out to see what it is? They will have to give you anesthesia.[9] Do you want that? It's okay, if you do, Grandma. Do you?

VIRGINIA: No. No.

(Frustration on her face.)

I don't . . . know.

(Lynn strokes her hair.)

LYNN: That's okay. It's okay, Grandma.

(Kisses her, then moves away from the bed and motions Beverly to follow.)

She's eighty-seven years old. She has a bad heart. When they put that telescope down her throat it will have to pass by her heart. She already has an irregular—

BEVERLY: The doctor hasn't reported that.

LYNN: She's been on heart meds for the last five years![10]

BEVERLY: She's not on any now.

LYNN: Because he took her off them. He has an agenda—the biopsy.

BEVERLY: It's a simple procedure.

LYNN: For a healthy person, maybe. But, Grandma . . . the anesthesia alone could send her into cardiac arrest.[11] You've got to tell someone.

BEVERLY: I can't.

LYNN: No one is listening. I need your help.

BEVERLY: I can't help you.

LYNN: The biopsy isn't necessary.

BEVERLY: The doctor wants to know what type of cancer it is.[12]

LYNN: And then what?

BEVERLY: He wants to treat her.

LYNN: They won't be able to cut it out with surgery. She wouldn't survive that. She won't survive chemo or radiation, either. She's eighty-seven. Her heart is too weak.

BEVERLY (*Whispering*): I know. You're right. If it was my grandmother, I'd be saying the same thing.[13]

LYNN: Then help me.

BEVERLY: I can't help you.[14]

LYNN: You just said—

BEVERLY: I can't go against the doctor.

LYNN: Someone has to. He's wrong.

BEVERLY: I can't say that.

LYNN: I'm begging you to. Beverly, please help me stop the biopsy.[15]

BEVERLY: No one will listen to me.

LYNN: Please . . .

BEVERLY: I can't help you, I'm sorry.

LYNN: God almighty . . . This is a nightmare[16] . . . Why won't anyone listen? Someone has to stop this!

BEVERLY: I can't. I have three kids. I'm on my own. I just can't, you understand, I can't help you.[17]

VIRGINIA: Bonnie? Where are you?! Bonnie!

LYNN (*Going to her*): I'm here, Grandma. It's me, Lynn.

VIRGINIA: Bonnie, who are you talking to? Who's in the kitchen?

(*Lynn sits beside her on the bed.*)

LYNN: No one, Grandma. There's no one—

VIRGINIA: Goddamn it! Someone is in the kitchen!

LYNN (Gently): Grandma, you're in the hospital.

VIRGINIA: Why don't they leave? Drunk idiots! I want to close early . . .[18]

LYNN: Grandma . . .

VIRGINIA: Oh, God! Someone is shooting . . . I've been shot . . .[19] Bonnie! Where's Lynnie? Oh, God . . . where's Lynnie . . .

LYNN: I'm here Grandma . . . I'm okay . . . It's okay . . . I'm here . . .

(Rests her head on Virginia's chest and softly sobs.)

VIRGINIA: Lynnie . . .

(Strokes her hair.)

Don't cry . . . don't cry . . . Grandma's all right . . . it's all right . . .

(Beverly, fighting her emotions, backs out of the room.)

1. This is a very dynamic way to begin a scene—with a decision on the table and the implication that there are stakes involved in the decision.

2. The exposition is motivated here by Virginia's infirmity. The fact that the nurse is using low-context dialogue to talk to Virginia does a good deal to suggest how out of it Virginia is. Also, from the years of exposure to medical stories, we know that a biopsy isn't proposed unless cancer is suspected, so, without using the term itself, the word "cancer" is in the audience's mind.

3. We're getting a very clear sense of Beverly's repertoire of voices as a nurse—the firm voice to Lynn and the condescending voice to Virginia.

4. My bet is you don't need Lynn's "She would say yes to anything right now." Lynn's action is going to make this vivid. In fact, you might even get away with Lynn just shaking her head at Beverly and going straight for the line about the elephants. Both Beverly and the audience would get Lynn's point.

5. I love this line. Nice and specific and ridiculous, and the fact that Virginia nods yes vividly establishes Lynn's point.

6. You don't need to announce that Virginia's confused. We've just figured that out for ourselves.

7. You don't really need to have the whole line here. "You don't need to be a psychiatrist to—" would get the idea across as well. We know where this line is going and so does Beverly. If the audience knows where a line is going, you don't need to have the whole line said.

8. This is probably the first place where you might use the word "confused."

9. For those who doubt that you can write vividly without adjectives and adverbs, look at this passage. Not an adjective or adverb (except for "down") in sight, and yet this conveys a strong sense of Lynn's passion.

10. That Lynn is using medical shorthand—"heart meds" strongly suggests how familiar she has become with procedures and jargon, which also strong suggests how deeply involved she has been with her grandmother's case over the years. Very subtle exposition.

11. A more conventional writer, still in the grip of proper grade school grammar, would have written this line, "But the anesthesia alone could send Grandma into cardiac arrest." By fragmenting the line, introducing "Grandma" at the beginning, and then having her revise the sentence so that "Grandma" is the object of the sentence rather than the subject—"But, Grandma . . . the anesthesia alone could send her into cardiac arrest."—you convey the sense of a mind alive, forming her speech on the fly. Very crafty line.

12. You probably can get away with using the word "cancer" here, though I'll bet it isn't necessary. Between "biopsy" and the upcoming reference to radiation, the audience will certainly know what's being talked about. And certainly Lynn and Beverly know.

13. The fact that Beverly changes her voice by whispering suggests that she's shifting from the professional to the personal role.

14. You probably don't need to keep repeating "help you" and "help me"

throughout the rest of the scene. We know what "can't" refers to, by now.

15. You don't need Lynn to say that she's begging. It's evident. And you don't really need to say that what she wants stopped is the biopsy; you have already established that pretty well.

16. Again, you are having her make an explicit evaluation that is unnecessary. We can tell from her behavior that Lynn thinks this is a nightmare.

17. I have a hunch the line would be more effective if it were just, "Look, I have three kids. I'm on my own." We would figure out from that and the context that Beverly's afraid of challenging the authority of the doctors, that her job is at stake.

18. Virginia's disorientation and the incidental details revealed by her conversation with an imaginary Bonnie give us specific clues as to the nature of what Virginia's younger life was like. Mention of "the kitchen" and "closing early" and "drunk idiots" implies that she ran a restaurant and is accustomed to having some authority. The authority she used to enjoy and the lack of authority she has now is telling.

19. This opens intriguing questions—has she ever been shot? Was she in that dangerous an environment?

I've picked at the places where I think too much is stated, but there's some very strong stuff in here. Beverly's divided feelings come through; her moral dilemma is vivid—torn between her private sympathies and her professional loyalties. Lynn's dialogue—particularly the elephants line—lends her an intelligence and imagination that lifts her out of the generic role of aggrieved relative. And, as I say, the hints of Virginia's past add poignance to her position.

By J. Holtham

(A somewhat secluded corner of a department store. Hal, in his twenties and wearing a store uniform, is stocking toys. Marty, also in his twenties, comes up behind him and watches him.)

MARTY (*In a fake voice*): Excuse me. Do you work here?

HAL (*Without turning, or any enthusiasm*): Yeah.

MARTY: Where are your tampons?

HAL: Third aisle on your left.

MARTY: Can you show me?

HAL: It's the third aisle on your left.

MARTY: I mean, can you show me how to use them.[1]

    (*Hal turns and sees Marty, who bursts into laughter.*)

Oh, man! Oh, you should have seen your face. Oh, man!

HAL: Ha. You're a shit head.[2]

MARTY: I'm not the one in the snappy red vest.

HAL: They make me wear it.

MARTY: No. I like it. It brings out your eyes . . .

HAL: Fuck you. Aren't you supposed to be minding the store?[3]

MARTY: Boris the Spider-Man gave me the afternoon off.

HAL: What'd he do? Drop dead?

MARTY: Nah, he got a bunch of old *X-men* off some guy from the city for like half what they're worth, so he's feeling like he's king of the world. Fat-ass bastard. He's walking around on a cloud. I told him I had a dentist appointment.

HAL: Slick.

MARTY: So, let's blow. Go out to Pig's. I almost beat Charlie last night, but I scratched on the eight ball.[4] I wanna get my five bucks back.

HAL: I got, like, half an hour left.

MARTY: So. Skip.

HAL: Nah. I can't. Hang around.[5]

MARTY: I'll meet you up there.

HAL: I don't have a ride. My mom's got the car.

MARTY: What about Candy?

HAL: Working.

MARTY: Shit.

HAL: Just go. I'll catch up.

MARTY: You won't.

HAL: I will.

MARTY: You won't.

HAL: Then wait.

MARTY: Fine.

    (Hal goes back to stacking. Marty walks around. He looks at the toys. He grabs a toy ray-gun and shoot at Hal.)

HAL: Come on, quit it. I already did that stuff.

MARTY: Damn. All right.

HAL: I just spent, like, all morning over there.

MARTY: Fine, fine. Don't get your panties in a bunch.[6] Give a guy a red vest and all of a sudden . . .

HAL: This is my section. I'm responsible.

MARTY: They stuck you with the Barbies? Hey, maybe next week, you'll get promoted to board games or something.

HAL *(Joking)*: I wish.

MARTY: That's where the real money is.

    (Marty wanders off again. He tries to look at something, but accidentally knocks over a bunch of other things.)[7]

HAL: Jesus, Marty.

MARTY: It was an accident.

HAL: Don't go messing with this.

MARTY: I'm not your fucking kid.

HAL: Just go wait in the car.

MARTY: No, I'll fix it.

    (Marty begins putting things away. Hal goes back to what he was doing. When he thinks Hal isn't looking, Marty sticks the ray-gun into his pants, under his shirt. Hal turns and looks at him.)

What?

    (Hal motions for him to put it back.)

What?

HAL *(Through clenched teeth)*: Put it back.

MARTY: I got nothing.

HAL: I saw you. Put it back.

MARTY: What's your problem?

HAL: Just put it back, Marty. This isn't funny.

MARTY: I told you, man, I don't have anything.

HAL: I saw you. The gun. You got it in your pants.

MARTY: Oh, I got a gun in my pants. Just ask your mom.

HAL: I'm serious. Put it back.

MARTY: What the fuck do you care?[8]

HAL: This is my section.

MARTY: Oh, it's your section. You're the boss back here, right, right. I forgot. Whatever, Hal.

HAL: I'm responsible here, Marty. You gotta put it back.

MARTY: What? Are they gonna count?

HAL: There are cameras all over the place. You walk out of here and they're going to know.

MARTY: So? You didn't see it.

HAL: I'm standing right here.

MARTY: They're not going to care about a fucking toy gun.

HAL: They're going to care if I let you walk away with it.

MARTY: Well, if you'd just act like nothing's happening, they wouldn't know.

HAL: Just put it back. Don't be a dick.[9]

MARTY: Who's being a dick? I'm being a dick? It's a fucking ninety-nine cent toy.

HAL: Yeah, what do you want with it?

MARTY: I like it. It goes—

(*He imitates the sound of it, loudly.*)

HAL: Shh! Asshole!

MARTY: You're being the asshole here. It's not like they're going to fire you.[10]

HAL: I can get in a lot of trouble.

MARTY: Then so what? Fuck 'em.

HAL: I need this job, Marty.

MARTY: You'll get another one.

HAL: I just got this one. And I don't want to get fired. Just put it back. Look, I'll buy it for you. Okay?

MARTY: Fuck that.

HAL: Fuck what? You want to get me fired?

MARTY: This is a bullshit job. Like every other fucking job in this bullshit town. You gotta remember that. Before you go ordering people around in your "section." Like your shit doesn't stink.

HAL: And yours doesn't, either? Making five bucks an hour making sure twelve-year-olds pay for their *Avengers* comics? Yeah, that puts you at the top of the food chain.[11]

MARTY: Fuck you. Walk to Pig's.

(*He starts out.*)

HAL: Hey. Hey. Give me the gun.

MARTY: Get the fuck off me.

HAL: Give it! Security! SECURITY!

(*He and Marty start to tussle. Hal grabs the gun, and Marty gives him a hard shove, knocking him into the shelving. Toys fly. Hal grabs Marty and punches him. Marty punches Hal back. Hal falls down. Marty trashes the section.*)[12]

MARTY: It was a real pleasure shopping here.

1. Well, we don't need too much more to have a strong idea about the sophistication of Marty's sense of humor.

2. "You're a shit head" is something Hal would indeed be likely to say. On the other hand, since we in the audience have already come to a similar conclusion, perhaps there's room for a more surprising or more ironic line here?

3. This initially confused me a bit because the scene is set in a store. It isn't until a little later we get the clues that Hal and Marty are referring to a comic book store where Marty works.

4. We get to figure out that Pig's is a place where Marty and his friends shoot pool and down beers. From this, and the later comment about Hal's mother having the car, it isn't too far a stretch to imagining these guys as living at home and scraping by on subsistence jobs.

5. Marty had lied to get a break from his job at the comic book store. Hal feels an obligation to finish his shift, even if it means wearing a uniform he doesn't like. The contrast between their attitudes toward their jobs is nicely established.

6. "Don't get your panties . . . " is an old line. There's the opportunity here to come up with a new phrase.

7. The disruption of the display is a good use of the disruption of an object technique I discussed in Lesson 3.

8. Part of what is interesting in this scene is Hal's conscientiousness about a job that he obviously doesn't much like. He's not letting his friendship with Marty keep him from meeting his responsibilities. Marty's purpose, on the other hand, is to test the limits of the friendship.

9. Hal continues to try to reconcile his responsibilities with his friendship. Marty is doing what he can to make this as difficult as possible.

10. Hal calls Marty "a dick" and "an asshole" and Marty turns them back around at Hal. Hal sees these words as applying to someone who would purposely disrupt a friend at his workplace. Marty sees these words as applying to someone who is so rigid as to place primary importance on a trivial job as opposed to the bonds of friendship. That they can use the same epithets but have them mean different things is another suggestion of the growing gulf in their perspectives.

11. Nicely handled escalation.

12. Again, very strong use of the disruption of objects.

Part of what is interesting in this scene is that Hal chooses to maintain his professional demeanor even though the job is not one to which he can have much attachment. He wants to keep peace with Marty (witness his intention of paying for the gun Marty is stealing), but he refuses to let Marty pull him into behavior that would threaten his job. In a sense, this is a scene about one character moving beyond adolescence and another refusing to, and how this must lead to the destruction of a friendship.

6
LESSON
Responsibility and Appetite

I BROUGHT UP SHAW'S FORMULATION OF THE PRIVATE VERSUS THE professional life as an easy way of introducing a larger topic—the idea that drama may arise when different aspects of a character are at war with each other.

In this lesson, I want to move one step further. With a thanks to Shaw (You may go back to your seat now, George), I turn now to Sigmund Freud.

Don't worry. We're not going to swim in the deep end of this pool. I'm only going to bring up a few basic terms and ideas, some of which are probably sufficiently familiar to you that you'll lip-synch with me. Then I want to apply them to writing.

One of the basic Freudian concepts involves the dynamic between the superego and the id. The superego is the part of the personality that generates the injunctions to do what one *should* do.

I *should* do my homework. I *should* cut the grass. I *should* balance my checkbook. I *should* tell the truth, pay my debts, meet my obligations, treat people with kindness and honesty.

The superego also fires warning shots to remind one of what one *should not* do.

I *should not* sit in bus seats reserved for the elderly and handicapped. I *should not* press a drink on a recovering alcoholic. I *should not* put the moves on my best friend's spouse. I *should not* remain silent if I observe an injustice being done.

The id is the source for the impulses to do what one *wants* to do—and right now if possible (and even if it *isn't* possible, damn it).

Notice that the impulses for what one wants to do are often linked to the injunctions of what one should not do. (Hey, but my best friend's spouse is hot and interested.) The id keeps whipping up the prospect of short-term pleasures or advantages. To a large degree, the superego's job is to keep the reins on the id's desire to plunge. (The id wants you to gulp down that piece of chocolate cake. The superego flashes a mental picture of you this summer trying to cram too much you into too little bathing suit.)

Of course, people who live only by the dicta of their superegos aren't likely to have a lot of fun. It may not be prudent to jump into a fountain wearing a business suit on a sweltering day, but it might be just what the moment demands.

According to Freudian theory, the part of the personality that moderates the interaction between the superego and the id is the ego, the referee between the ongoing confrontation between responsibility and appetite.

It is this battle—between responsibility and appetite—that is at the center of the central character of many plays. Two recent biographical plays are built on exactly this model.

In William Luce's *Barrymore*, the actor for whom the play is named has rented a theatre for an evening in order to rehearse *Richard* III. His last chance to resurrect his career is to put together a credible performance in this, the role that had helped establish his reputation decades before. The responsible side of his character—the superego—urges him to rehearse, and every now and then he makes a stab at running some lines. The appetite side—his id—senses the presence of an audience and, desiring to entertain us (and himself), he capitulates to every possible distraction and temptation to recite bawdy limericks and tell anecdotes about his family, ex-wives, and friends. The point of Luce's play is that ultimately John Barrymore hasn't got the strength of character to live up to his potential as an artist. Good and amusing company he is, yes (especially in Christopher Plummer's flamboyant performance), but, because his appetite for mischief and his desire to ingratiate overwhelm his sense of responsibility to his art, he is doomed. And he knows it.

In Pam Gems' *Stanley*, painter Stanley Spencer maintains his responsibility to his art, continuing to produce canvas after canvas. But he is unable to withstand the temptation of Patricia, an unscrupulous, fortune-hunting would-be artist, who demands that he discard his adored and adoring wife to make her (Patricia) the second Mrs. Spencer. Here again the triumph of appetite over responsibility leads to disaster. (Stanley is so headlong in his infatuation with Patricia that he doesn't quite notice that she is a lesbian, hardly a promising marital partner for a heterosexual male.) Gems' play makes the intriguing case that the impulses that give Stanley's paintings their vitality spring from the same source as the impulses that lead him to make a mess of his life.

In fact, it is often appetite that makes a character memorable. Another Stanley—Kowalski—seems to want to devour the world in Tennessee Williams' A *Streetcar Named Desire*. If *Gypsy's* Mama Rose had a stronger superego, perhaps she would suppress her yen for showbiz, marry Herbie, and give her daughters the stable childhood they desire. The young black imposter in John Guare's *Six Degrees of Separation* pursues access to the good life and immediate sexual gratification with a heedlessness that disrupts (sometimes to the point of destruction) everyone with whom he comes into contact.

The deck isn't always stacked against the superego in theatre and film, though. In the musical *Hair* and other works expressing the spirit of the 1960s, the tales often center on people whose lives till now have been dominated by their killjoy superegos; typically they run into the id people (often hippies and other such "natural" types) and are liberated or go through experiences that allow them to liberate themselves. The image is often one of escape. In *The Graduate*, Benjamin and Elaine flee the restrictive and hypocritical world of their parents. In I *Love You, Alice B. Toklas*, the button-down character played by Peter Sellers abandons his conventional fiancée to find his authentic self. The authors of that script, Paul Mazursky and Larry Tucker, went one step further with their screenplay for *Bob and Carol and Ted and Alice*, in which two conventional bourgeois couples *try* to junk their superegos because, uh, they think they should. (A lovely contradiction in terms. They feel that they *should* junk the part of them that says what they should and should not do. The id has *become* the superego. Which is one of the reasons the piece is a successful satire.)

These days, it is in comedies that giving free expression to impulse is most often celebrated. In their most successful films, Robin Williams, Jim Carrey, Bill Murray, Eddie Murphy, Whoopi Goldberg, and John Belushi have given voice to the audience's desire to violate inhibiting social codes. The reason most of these pictures end on a slightly disappointing note is that, though these performers misbehave for the bulk of the picture, by the fade-out they almost always make peace with society and prove themselves to be good citizens at heart.

The other figures who act most exuberantly on impulse tend to be the villains, which is why In the Line of Fire's John Malkovich, Die Hard's Alan Rickman, Schindler's List's Ralph Fiennes, Goodfellas' Joe Pesci, Under Siege's Tommy Lee Jones, Speed's Dennis Hopper, and Rob Roy's Tim Roth tend to be more fun to watch than the leads of those pictures. (Of course, they all end up dead. Hmm.)

As I mentioned earlier in this book, Shakespeare dramatized the battle vividly in Henry IV, Parts 1 and 2. Much of the action of these works involves pitting the superego ethic of the dour and rigid king who gives the plays their titles against the exuberant personification of the id that is Sir John Falstaff. Their contrasting physiques underscore the difference—the king is gaunt with care, Falstaff is fat from his incapacity to deny himself. It is Henry who speaks constantly to his son Hal of honor. It is to Falstaff that Shakespeare gives the famous passage debunking it:

FALSTAFF: Can honour set-to a leg? No. Or an arm? No. Or take away the grief of a wound? No. Honour hath no skill in surgery, then? No. What is honour? A word. What is in that word, honour? Air. A trim reckoning! Who hath it? He that died o' Wednesday. Doth he feel it? No. Doth be hear it? No. 'Tis insensible then? Yea, to the dead. But will it not live with the living? No. Why? Detraction will not suffer it. Therefore I'll none of it. Honour is a mere scutcheon—and so ends my catechism.

Ultimately, after the deaths of both Henry IV (his biological father) and Falstaff (his surrogate father), Hal incorporates the best of both and becomes as perfect an image of man as Shakespeare ever drew.

I suggest that if you're faced with an impasse in the development of the central character of your current work, you might want to ask yourself what resides in these two corners of his or her personality. What does your lead believe to be the behavior to which one should subscribe in order to support order and the long-term good? What are the short-term hungers that entice him or her to stray from the path mapped out by conscience?

The key to the solution of your dramatic problem may lie in finding the civil war between responsibility and appetite that is in the heart of your protagonist.

> **Assignment Six:** Compose a scene in which your central character is torn between appetite and responsibility.

By *Martha Humphreys*

> *(Angel Caruthers' bedroom, a frilly room decorated in pastels and floral patterns. Present are Angel Caruthers and Linda McKenzie. Both are 17. Angel is petite and very pretty. Linda is a larger, plainer girl. They are sitting on the bed with an open box of doughnuts between them.)*

LINDA: But she's my best friend.[1]

ANGEL: You'll have new best friends. Crystal and Lindsey really want you to join.

LINDA: I see Alice every day. We have all our classes together.

ANGEL: Le Club is not a class.[2]

LINDA: I know that. It's just that . . . Well, Alice is my best friend.

ANGEL: You said that. You want a doughnut?[3]

LINDA: No. I have to fit into that dress. The dance is only five days away.

ANGEL: Eric taking you?

LINDA: Yes.

ANGEL: You know he only dates members of Le Club.

LINDA: He asked me out.

ANGEL: Once. Have you finished that history project?

LINDA: Alice and I are working on it together.

ANGEL: Oh.

LINDA: She's a real good student. Give her a chance. You'd like her. She's got a real good sense of humor.

ANGEL: Who's she been dating?

LINDA: Timothy Clayburn.

ANGEL: Isn't he president of something?

LINDA: The chess club.

ANGEL: That's the game with horses?[4]

LINDA: Knights.

ANGEL: Whatever. You sure you don't want a doughnut?

LINDA: Yes.

ANGEL: I don't think Eric's into chess. Football takes up so much time. You know he dated Cherry Yates last year?

LINDA: The cheerleader?

(Angel nods.)

Is she in Le Club?

ANGEL: She was.

LINDA: She dropped out?

ANGEL: Not exactly. Her father lost his job. They had to move. She doesn't really live near us anymore.

LINDA: And Eric broke up with her?

ANGEL: Yep.

(A doorbell rings.)

LINDA: Who's that?

ANGEL: Probably Crystal and Lindsey. They said they might come over. Just to talk. They really want to get to know you. Come on. It's not like you're joining right now.

LINDA: All right.

ANGEL: Last chance for a doughnut.

LINDA: Well, maybe half.[5]

---

1. Nothing says that a scene has to start with someone making an entrance. You often don't need the greetings and exchange of pleasantries with which people begin most conversations. The

audience has been trained, through years of film and TV, to accept beginning a sequence later in the action. Mamet uses this technique more often than not. Look at the three scenes in the first act of *Glengarry Glen Ross*; in each, we join the pairs of characters in the middle of their encounter. Sometimes, as in the case with this scene, the first line is very explicitly a reaction to a previous line we are invited to imagine. The fact that we are invited to imagine it means that the audience is instantly engaged in analysis and so is immediately involved in the action of the scene. In this case, the line, "But she's my best friend" instantly suggests that whatever Angel is proposing to Linda is something that could be seen as a betrayal of a friendship.

2. Angel is making a false distinction, which offers a sense of what the general level of her tactics is likely to be.

3. Angel's temptation of Linda with the doughnut is a parallel to her temptation of Linda away from her friendship with Alice. And the objections Linda raises supports the idea that, in both the cases of the doughnut and the renunciation of Alice, Linda is conscious of where her higher choices lie.

4. Angel's ignorance of and disdain for chess suggests an anti-intellectual disposition. There are other clues in the scene that Le Club's membership are less interested in who has brains than who has money. Of course, the fact that the group calls itself Le Club implies its immaturity and affectation.

5. Linda's acceptance of half the doughnut signals that she will probably try initially to balance her membership in Le Club with her friendship with Alice. But I think we're left suspecting that she will capitulate and eat the whole doughnut just as she will eventually capitulate and dump Alice. And, yes, she probably will have trouble getting into that dress for the dance, which will further damage her self-respect. I bet I'm not alone in suspecting that this is a setup, that Le Club just wants to wreak havoc on Linda to provide them amusement, and that, after Linda has ruined her friendship with Alice, they'll probably keep her out of Le Club anyway.

By Kristine Niven

(Night. The porch of a suburban house. A brittle wreath sits on the front door. Joan, about 35, and Jessie, 14 years old, arrive together from the street. They are in mid-conversation.)

JESSIE: Would you let *me* sleep in a backseat?

JOAN: I let you sleep in a tent in the backyard when you were six.[1]

JESSIE: You wouldn't and you know it.

JOAN: I understand your concerns and I love you for it. Okay? Now bring me a blanket from the hall closet.[2]

JESSIE: They're not there any more. She keeps them in the TV room, sorry, her "studio."[3]

JOAN: She's an artist?

(Jessie lifts the wreath from the center of the door and shows it to Joan.)

JESSIE: What do you call this?[4]

(She shoves the wreath into Joan's hands. Being brittle, pieces of the wreath begin to crumble as Joan holds it.)
Staying in my room isn't like going in the whole house. It's *my* room.

JOAN: How am I supposed to get *to* your room?[5]

(She tries to rehang the wreath, but pieces continue to fall off.)

JESSIE: Shall I bring you out a roll of toilet paper, or do you carry it with you?[6]

JOAN: Jessie, I cannot come in the house. I promised.

(Joan gives up on the wreath and hands what's left to Jessie.)

JESSIE: You haven't even seen my room in over a year!

JOAN: Honey, I remember every inch. I see it with my eyes shut.

JESSIE: Actually, I've redone most of it.

JOAN: Is that so?

JESSIE: I painted one corner pure black and I've written verses from Marilyn Manson next to my Ozzy Osborne poster.

JOAN: Ah, right next to Princess Leia and the Wookies.[7]

(Jessie drops the wreath and opens the door.)

JESSIE: Come on, I'll show you.

JOAN: I promised your father.[8]

JESSIE: They won't be back until late tomorrow.

JOAN: A promise is a promise. How would you feel if I broke a promise to you?

JESSIE: How would you feel if I got drunk![9]

JOAN: Oh, Jessie. . . .

JESSIE: I could, you know. Being in this house all alone. I could get scared and open a bottle of wine. Drink the whole thing.

JOAN: Since when do you like wine?

JESSIE: Maybe I've learned to like it. Maybe I'm so scared it doesn't matter if I like it or not. I might even drink two bottles.

JOAN: Make sure it's the good stuff, the more expensive the better.[10]

JESSIE: One call to a cell phone and I could have 10, 20 kids here. They'd bring their own beer, too. I think Leo just scored some stuff. It's time I learned to smoke, don't you think?

JOAN: It's not all it's cracked up to be. Whoa, there's a joke!

JESSIE: You don't think I'm serious.

JOAN: Jessie. . . .

JESSIE: I've been left all alone in this house, with nobody watching out for me.

JOAN: Your father obviously trusts you.

JESSIE: My father can't be bothered coming up with an alternative.

(Joan reaches to touch Jessie's face. Jessie ducks her mother's hand.)

Did I tell you she nailed my window shut?[11]

JOAN: Nailed your—

JESSIE: Window . . . shut! She made Dad drive four-inch nails into the sill so I can't open it. She thinks I sneak out.

JOAN: I . . . I . . . um . . . why would you do that?

JESSIE: I *wouldn't!*!! Look, she nails my window shut one day and the next she's leaving me alone overnight. Ma, they won't know if you come in the house or not. She'll probably think you did anyway, so why not! Dad's probably already forgotten the promise.

JOAN: I haven't forgotten it. It's a promise. I never back down on my word and neither do you. We don't do that.

JESSIE: "Love, honor . . . obey?"[12]

JOAN: Oh, criminey . . .

JESSIE: It's all right to break some promises and not others? Tell me, Mother, how am I supposed to figure out which ones are breakable and which are not?

JOAN: I still love and honor your father.

JESSIE: Right. And that's why I'm stuck with this teenager for a step-monster.

JOAN: There's a lot you don't know, a lot you can't understand right now.

JESSIE: Geez—

JOAN: I love you and I wouldn't do anything to—

JESSIE: Yada yada, blah blah blah.

JOAN: Jessie . . .

JESSIE: Ma, I'm getting cold. Will you come inside so we can get some sleep?

JOAN: Bring me out a blanket . . . please . . . and a pillow.

JESSIE: I'll call the cops. I'm serious. I will do it.

JOAN: Of course you will.

JESSIE: I'll tell them I'm alone . . . a kid . . . and someone's outside. The neighbors will see the police lights, see you being hauled off.

JOAN: They don't haul off mothers watching over their kids.

JESSIE: "My parents aren't here. I don't know who this woman is, Officer."

JOAN: Well, that would certainly get me a bed for the night.

JESSIE: Okay. Stay outside. I don't care. Sleep in the car, piss in the bushes, put a goddamn paper cup on the sidewalk! I don't care!

(*Swings open the door and goes inside. Joan wavers, then steps inside the house and closes the door. The lock clicks shut.*)[13]

1. Joan's comment about "letting her" sleep in the backyard instantly establishes that she's Jessie's mother.

2. Good introduction of the object—the blanket. We begin to suspect that the issue of sleeping in the backseat is related to the request for the blanket. And perhaps we begin to put together why Jessie's mother would sleep in the car in front of the house that is apparently Jessie's home.

3. Ah, the introduction of "she." We're beginning to put together the circumstances: Jessie's house is not Joan's house, which means that Joan and Jessie's father are no longer together. That this used to be Joan's house (and pretty recently) is underscored by Joan's knowing that the blankets are in the hall closet. Except they aren't. "She" has put them in the TV room, which is now her studio. So, "she" has changed the house. And we figure that "she" is probably a stepmother. This is very smart work and anticipates a technique I'll be discussing in Lesson 9—high-context exposition.

4. The introduction of another object—the wreath, which represents the presence of "she" on the stage. What happens to the wreath later speaks volumes about Jessie's feelings and Joan's discomfort.

5. This makes strong use of the negotiation of space, which I discussed in Lesson 4.

6. Jessie's introduction of a hypothetical object, the toilet paper, is a very efficient way of getting across the impracticality of Joan's plan.

7. The contrast in the posters suggests (a) the angry image Jessie is trying to project, and (b) the aspect of Jessie that Joan remembers and suspects is still dominant in her daughter's character.

8. The promise to her father begins to suggest the way that Joan's relationship to her ex complicates her relationship with her daughter.

9. Nice echoing of the phrase, "How would you feel—" In conversation, we frequently reply with elements of what the other person has said. Of course, in this line, Jessie is beginning her appeal to her mother's sense of maternal responsibility for a daughter who has been left all alone in the house. She's trying to make Joan's feelings for her over-

whelm Joan's desire to keep faith with her ex by not going into the house when he's not there.

10. This passage nicely juxtaposes Jessie's various threats of bad behavior with Joan's implicit statements of confidence in her daughter's good judgment.

11. Nice vivid image that further supports Jessie's implied claim of the stepmother's nuttiness.

12. We recognize this instantly as being the traditional (if outmoded) wedding vows. Jessie bringing this up at this point suggests that the end of the marriage was something that Joan brought about. Again, very nice use of the implicit.

13. Always effective to have a decision made evident by an action rather than an announcement.

Joan is indeed torn between her sense of responsibility—keeping her word to her ex—and her appetite—spending the evening close to her daughter. This is further complicated by the fact that her appetite is also linked with another responsibility: she probably believes that fourteen-year-old Jessie is too young to have been left alone in the house by her ex and his new wife, and she feels, yes, that as a mother she *should* be there to protect and take care of Jessie.

This is a very rich little scene. What I especially like is that it puts the audience into the position of being as conflicted as Joan herself is. Most people like to think of themselves as honorable people, people who keep their promises. At what point is it appropriate to break a promise? And the scene is heightened by the fact that apparently Joan was the one who broke up the marriage and so broke the promise she made at the ceremony, so trying to maintain an appearance of integrity before both her daughter and herself is understandably even more important to her.

7

LESSON

Different Relationships, Different Roles

WHAT I HAVE BEEN ADDRESSING IN THE LAST TWO LESSONS IS what, in *The Dramatist's Toolkit*, I call "roles in conflict." In Lesson 5, the roles were professional and personal ones. In Lesson 6, they were defined by the competing pulls of responsibility and appetite. (Notice how these may overlap: one's responsibility may stem from a professional identity and one's appetite from a personal desire.) Now I want to expand the discussion to a more general exploration of this concept.

In scene three of my play, *With and Without*, Glen tells Jill how his recent divorce has made him modify his behavior.

GLEN: . . . . . I've noticed it's changed the way I answer the phone.

JILL: How did you used to answer the phone?

GLEN (*Lightly*): Hello?

JILL: And now?

GLEN (*Neutrally*): Hello?

JILL: And that's why?

GLEN: Well, it could be her. Don't want to answer (*Lightly*) "Hello?" if it's her.

JILL: You afraid that she'll think that you're happy?

GLEN: I say it that way and it's her, I have to do a whole readjustment thing.

JILL (*Darkly*): What—"Oh, it's you?"

GLEN: Like in music, a modulation to a different key.

JILL: Major to minor?

GLEN: I do the modulation too abruptly, she gets offended and pissed off. So I do this more neutral "hello."

JILL: This leaves you positioned to modulate to whatever key you want.

GLEN: Maximum flexibility.

This passage is based on the observation that, when you answer the phone, you speak with a neutral tone until the party calling you identifies him- or herself. When you know to whom you are speaking, you switch to the voice that is appropriate to that person. If you're like me, sometimes you're aware of the click of that appropriate voice locking in (particularly when you answer the phone expecting to hear one person on the other end of the line and instead are greeted by another for whom you have different feelings). Each of us has a repertory of voices. Each of the voices in our repertory is linked to another role we play, and every person in our life elicits from us the voice affiliated with the role we play with that person.

What's more, every role is linked to a different objective, and each objective prompts a different train of behavior. Sometimes these trains go in different directions; sometimes those roles are irreconcilable. The behavior urged by pursuing the objective associated with one role comes into conflict with the behavior urged by pursuing the objective associated with another.

Premise for a script: Till now, Marilyn's life has been without romance. She's looked after her father, a retired professor of mathematics, since her mother died. Now in her forties, she meets a plumber named Hal and falls in love. Marilyn and Hal begin to talk of marriage. But her father is a snob and can't stand her beau, and there's little love lost from Hal's side.

Marilyn's father brings out in her the imperative to be his caregiver, and Hal brings out the imperatives of a would-be lover. Father appeals to the side that correlates status with education; Hal appeals to the side in which the practical dominates. Try as she might, Marilyn can't fulfill the roles of both daughter-caregiver and lover. How she tries to simultaneously satisfy father and boyfriend would be the basis of the early parts of the story. Their competing claims to her loyalty and affection would trigger a civil war in her heart. Ultimately, she would have to choose which is her higher or truer role. The resolution of this tale, then, would depend on which role she chose to assume. The audience watching this story would wait to see what action she takes. Inherent in that would be the choice of who she decides to be.

The contest between the roles can't be dramatically compelling, of course, unless there are powerful reasons driving the central character to embrace each. If the choice between roles is easy, then there's no contest to be played out.

In tragedy, the choice is often between an ignominious option that promises survival and the noble option which promises destruction. In Robert Bolt's A Man for All Seasons, Sir Thomas More doesn't *want* to be a martyr. He keeps trying to find technical ways of not speaking up against Henry VIII's plan to divorce so that he (More) can simultaneously claim his conscience and keep his head. Ultimately, however, he can't reconcile these objectives. Choosing conscience, he takes the path that leads to the axe.

And, indeed, along the way we are witness to various of More's voices. In scenes with Henry VIII, he speaks as a wary friend who knows his friendship is disposable if he becomes a political obstacle. He speaks with an informal and affectionate voice with his wife, and with a highly formal voice when he stands in front the tribunal that will condemn him to death. Bolt places More in different contexts specifically to elicit More's different sides and drives and, yes, voices.

Frequently the different faces of a character will be underscored by differences in dress. Bolt used this technique in his screenplay for David Lean's film, *Lawrence of Arabia* (which also included material by blacklisted screenwriter Michael Wilson). In early scenes, the young T. E. Lawrence is introduced whiling away time in an army office wearing the short khaki pants of a low-ranking officer's uniform. Dispatched as a liaison to the Arabs, Lawrence distinguishes himself and is rewarded by the Arabs with the flowing white robes of a chief. (There is a delightful scene of him newly robed, boyishly relishing the moves he can make in his new costume.) Late in the picture, having failed in his attempts to bring the various tribes together in a united Arab state, he gives up his robes. The last view we have of him is riding in a jeep, once again in a British officer's uniform. He looks as if he has shrunk. Part of the point of the film is that he can't be both a British officer and an Arab nationalist; he cannot reconcile these two aspects of his character.

In *Bluff*, within the space of a few pages, I had the opportunity to bring out three different voices of Emily in conversation with three other characters. Here's the setup for the first scene: While entertaining a young lady of brief acquaintance named Bonnie in his Greenwich Village apartment, Neal hears a commotion outside. He looks out his window, sees a gay-bashing in progress, throws on a coat, grabs a bat, and runs downstairs. The assailants take off, and Emily, a young woman passing on the street, joins Neal to look after the victim, Loring. At this point in the play, Bonnie has absented herself, and Emily and Neal are sitting in a hospital waiting for news on whether Loring is OK.

EMILY: You mind my asking a question?

NEAL: Something personal and private?

EMILY: What else is worth asking?

NEAL: No, she isn't.

EMILY: I didn't think so.

NEAL: We met tonight at a party.

EMILY: So, tonight was what?

NEAL: It never got to the "what" stage. Not quite.

EMILY: Hence your lack of shirt under the coat. And your lack of belt.

NEAL: They probably have a coffee machine around here.

EMILY: A couple more questions. If you don't mind.

NEAL: Do I get to ask you some?

EMILY: Oh, is there something you want to know?

NEAL: Why you're asking me these questions.

EMILY: Maybe I'm curious as to what's what.

NEAL: And what use would you make of this information?

EMILY: A person can only act on the basis of what they believe circumstances to be.

NEAL: You're investigating circumstances.

EMILY: Yes.

NEAL: Should I then infer you are contemplating action of some sort?

EMILY: You're teasing me.

NEAL: You make it pretty hard for me not to.

EMILY: Did you say something about a coffee machine?

NEAL: I met Bonnie tonight at a party. I invited her back to my place for purposes I'm sure it won't strain your imagination to, uh—

EMILY: Imagine?

NEAL: Confirmation that this idea was agreeable to her was in the process of being—

EMILY: Expressed?

NEAL: —expressed, yes, when Loring started getting the shit beat out of him.

EMILY: Leading you to pick up your baseball bat.

NEAL: Well, even when you have a hard-on, sometimes priorities are clear.

EMILY (*Not turning a hair*): Good to know.

NEAL: And no, when I invited Bonnie to my place, it was not in the expectation that this would begin a substantial and meaningful chapter in my life. And she was pretty clear about her interests being strictly—

EMILY: —recreational?

NEAL (*Nodding*):—recreational.

EMILY: How do you discriminate, uh, distinguish between people with purely recreational potential and—

NEAL: And?

EMILY: —those with whom you—

NEAL: Well, how does it work for you? Say, you see somebody—you're interested or not on the basis of what?

EMILY (*A beat, then—*): I'm not going to say looks don't count. Not just looks, as in handsome or not. But bearing, demeanor.

NEAL: Poise?

EMILY: Poise, yes.

NEAL: And standing there without my shirt and belt, you thought I was poiseful?

EMILY: Oh yes.

NEAL: Are you seeing somebody or are you also in a recreational phase?

EMILY (*Overlapping*): Nothing's going on that would be a serious impediment.

NEAL: Dinner tomorrow night?

EMILY: I would like to make something clear: I am not a Bonnie.

Later in the play, we see Emily speaking long-distance with her mother, Georgia, who is in another hospital. After their conversation, she has a short exchange with her stepfather, Gene.

GEORGIA: Don't be silly.

EMILY: I could get some time off from work. . . . . . I could take a week off, fly out.

GEORGIA: Thank you, honey, but no—I'm fine.

EMILY: I'm still not clear about what happened.

GEORGIA: I don't know, it's a vitamin thing.

EMILY: Vitamin?

GEORGIA: Too much of this, too little of that.

EMILY: And that put you into the hospital?

GEORGIA: Well, I got dizzy and fell down and got banged up a little. How did you find out I was here anyway?

EMILY: Noli called me.

GEORGIA: Noli should keep her nose on her own side of the fence.

EMILY: She did what you or Gene should have done. I was under the impression that I'm a member of this family. That somebody might think to call me about it when stuff that's important happens.

GEORGIA: But that's the point—it really isn't all that important.

EMILY: You're in the hospital.

GEORGIA: Lots of people are in the hospital. Why don't you call *them*?

EMILY: Lots of people aren't my mom.

GEORGIA: Well right now, if you don't mind, your mom would like to go to the little girl's room.

EMILY: Is Gene there?

GEORGIA: Why?

EMILY: Put him on.

GEORGIA: Don't you give him a hard time.

EMILY: I want to talk to him.

GEORGIA: Gene?

> (*Gene, in his fifties or sixties, appears.*)

She's going to give you a hard time.

> (*Gene takes the phone as Georgia exits.*)

GENE: What, did Noli call you?

EMILY: What is this about vitamins? She said something about this being about vitamins?

GENE: She's going to be all right.

EMILY: The way she talked, it sounded like scurvy.

GENE: She could pay better attention to what she eats.

EMILY: And what she drinks?

GENE: She tell you that?

EMILY: What do you think?

GENE: It's under control.

EMILY: Then why is she in the hospital?

GENE: She had an accident. Anybody can have an accident.

EMILY: But accidents are more likely to happen under certain circumstances.

> (*A beat.*)

GENE: I'll be coming to New York for a convention about the first week of October. You be in town then?

EMILY: Yes.

GENE: See you then.

EMILY: Call me if there's anything I should—

GENE: I will.

Emily's voice with Neal is one she employs to signal an interest in the possibility of a romantic relationship. There is a playful archness to her speech, a mock formality that she uses to let him know she is as educated as he is and as candid about sexual matters. With Georgia, the playfulness is gone, replaced by a directly expressed concern. With Gene, the tone shifts again to one of implicit criticism and reproof. (As you may have noticed, in neither the conversation with Georgia nor Gene do I use the words "alcohol" or "drinking problem.")

> **Assignment Seven:** Write two short scenes. Scene one will feature characters A and B. Scene two will feature characters A and C. That is to say, one character will appear in both scenes. The scenes are designed to bring out different sides of A. (For instance, the first scene might be about Jones talking to his boss. The second might be about Jones talking to his bookie. Obviously, Jones will talk differently to these two.) The idea is to show the same character in two different contexts that, in a full-length work, might set up the choice that would provide the central issue of the story.

By Richard Warren

Scene One

(*Sara's bedroom. Sara, five, is taking clothes out of a dresser as Bill, her father, enters.*)

BILL: What you up to?

SARA: Packing.

BILL: Packing?

SARA: Packing to go.

BILL: Go where?

SARA: Packing to go see Mickey Mouse.

BILL: That's not for a whole week, sweetheart.[1]

SARA: I'm packing to go.

BILL: It's next week.

SARA: I want to see Mickey Mouse.

BILL: Me too.

SARA: And Donald Duck and Minnie Mouse and Bugs Bunny and Goofy.

BILL: Bugs Bunny's not there.

SARA: You said.

BILL: I didn't say Bugs Bunny was there.

SARA: You said I could see everyone.

BILL: You can see everyone.

SARA: I want to see Bugs Bunny.

BILL: Bugs Bunny doesn't live there.

SARA: Where's he live?

BILL: I don't know.

SARA: I want to go to where Bugs Bunny lives.

BILL: I'll try to find out where he lives, and then we'll see.

SARA: I want to go to where Bugs Bunny lives.

BILL: I said, "We'll see."

SARA: Do you want to see Bugs Bunny?

BILL: If we can.

SARA: Judy does.

BILL: Did she say that?

SARA: Judy said she wants to see Bugs Bunny.

BILL: Who else did she say she wanted to see?

SARA: Just Bugs Bunny she said.

BILL: No one else?

SARA: She didn't say anyone else . . . Is Judy packing?

BILL: I don't know whether she's packing yet, but she will.

SARA: Do you love Judy?

BILL: Yes, I love Judy.[2]

SARA: As much as me?

BILL: I love Judy different. You're daddy's little girl. Daddy's little Sara, so I love you a lot.[3]

SARA: How much?

BILL: A lot. Lots and lots.

SARA: Do you love Judy lots and lots?

BILL: I love Judy different.

SARA: But not lots and lots.

BILL: Just different, that's all. Just different.

SARA: Are you going to sit beside me?[4]

BILL: Sit beside you?

SARA: When we go on rides.

BILL: Rides?

SARA: When we see Mickey Mouse. The scary rides.

BILL: Of course. I'll sit beside you.

SARA: And hold me?

BILL: And hold you.

SARA: So I won't be scared?

BILL: So you won't be scared.

SARA: And not Judy.

BILL: And not Judy?

SARA: Hold me and not Judy.

BILL: I thought you liked Judy.

SARA: You're going to hold me.

BILL: I can hold both of you. One on each side.

SARA: You're going to hold me tightest because I'm littlest.

BILL: Who's going to hold Daddy? What if Daddy gets scared?

SARA: I'm going to hold you.

BILL: Real tight?

SARA: Real tight.[5]

Scene Two

(Bill and his girlfriend, Judy, are having drinks at her apartment.)

JUDY: What do you want from me? I said, "I'm sorry."

BILL: Sorry?

JUDY: I just can't do it.

BILL: You said, "OK." You gave me the green light.

JUDY: So?

BILL: So what's the problem?

JUDY: I can't take the week.[6]

BILL: You knew it was a week. I told you it was. Didn't I tell you it was?

JUDY: Yes. So . . .

BILL: So I planned it with your blessing.

JUDY: Blessing. My blessing? Jesus Christ. You make it sound like we're planning a pilgrimage to the Vatican, for Christ's sake. Some religious experience. It's Disney World, fucking Disney World we're talking about. And frankly Bill, I'm a little old for Disney World.

BILL: They have adult stuff. Stuff to do at night.

JUDY: What are you planning on doing with Sara?

BILL: We can get a sitter. For after she's in bed.

JUDY: And what about when she's not in bed?

BILL: We'll be with her. In Fantasyland and Tomorrowland. Maybe riding Space Mountain and going through Toad Hall. Pirates of the Caribbean. All that stuff . . . And let's not forget the Haunted House. You'll love the Haunted House. Wooooo.

JUDY: We'll never know because I'm not going to the Haunted House. I'm not blowing a week at Disney World.

BILL: Sara's counting on it. She's already packing.

JUDY: She can go. You can go. I'm not stopping you. It's just that I'm not going.

BILL: She's counting on you going. You told her you were going.

JUDY: I said I'd think about it. And now I've thought about it, and I'm not going.

BILL: I thought you liked Sara.

JUDY: I like Sara. Did I say I didn't like Sara?

BILL: This is a chance for us to get away together. All of us. Like a family.

JUDY: Like a family?[7]

BILL: Yes. Like a family. I thought that was where we were headed.

JUDY: Is that what this is about?

BILL: What?

JUDY: You're looking for a mother for Sara.

BILL: No.

JUDY: No? That's what it sounds like to me.

BILL: I told you I had a daughter. Right up front I told you that. Sara was no surprise.

JUDY: Bill, I'm an executive. A vice president. I work hard. I get very little time off. And the very little time off I get I'm not spending at Disneyland.[8]

BILL: Disney World.

JUDY: I said, "Disney World."

BILL: No. You said, "Disneyland."

JUDY: Land. World. Big fucking deal. The point's the same. I'm not going.

BILL: Sara's counting on you going.

JUDY: She'll get over it. She's got to be disappointed sometime. Wait till she finds out Santa Claus is bogus.

BILL: I bet you can't wait to be the first to tell her.[9]

JUDY: I think you got the message. Now do you want to sneak out and get a bite to eat or do you want to strip down and hit the sack?[10]

BILL: I think I want to go home.

JUDY: Suit yourself.[11]

1. Nice organic way of suggesting a trip has been planned. Also, though neither "Disneyland" or "Disney World" has been mentioned, we can figure out the plan is to go to one of those, especially since a world where, as we discover shortly, Bugs Bunny (a Warner Brothers character) doesn't live.

2. This establishes that Judy is Bill's girlfriend.

3. I think that this is—if you'll pardon the expression in this context— Mickey Mousing. We've figured out by now that she's Daddy's little girl, and I think we don't need this to be said overtly. It sounds like the writer trying to make something completely clear for the audience.

4. The question of which one of them—Sara or Judy—Bill is going to sit beside on the rides nicely suggests Sara's competitiveness.

5. The only reservation I have about this scene is that Bill is so completely indulgent as a father during this. Mind you, this is a matter of taste, but I would have liked to have seen some indication of the effort he puts into maintaining this tone with his daughter, perhaps having to rephrase something that comes out a little overtly impatient. But I emphasize, this is a matter of taste.

6. By here, we figure out that Judy and Bill are debating a plan he thought was settled.

7. And now we're getting to the really meaty part of the scene. Judy's response—reinforced by her subsequent lines—makes clear that the two different perspectives on the proposed trip to Disney World are coming from two different perspectives on what Judy and Bill think this relationship is about or could be about.

8. Very interesting that Judy doesn't follow up on the question of her relationship with Sara but with her status as an exec.

9. This line reinforces the idea that Bill now sees Judy as a carrier of disillusionment.

10. A new plan proposed by Judy, which emphasizes her priorities and underscores what she wants out of the relationship.

11. Sounds like these two are on the verge of breaking up.

This is a very craftily composed pair of scenes. Certainly they illustrate Bill's divided loyalties, which could be the basis of a workable piece. Each of these ladies wants Bill on her own terms and wants him to declare his priorities. Most of the discussion is about differing plans for how Judy is to spend her week's vacation. I like very much that the phrase "single father" is never used. I like, too, that Bill never explicitly talks about his hope that he will marry Judy. Most of the dialogue in these scenes relates to discussions about concrete choices to be made in the near future, and from them we get a sense of the dynamics of these relationships. We also get a sense of what the backstory might be.

8

LESSON

Different Roles Within a Relationship

IN THE BRILLIANT 1960 SECOND CITY SCENE, "FIRST AFFAIR," developed improvisationally by Barbara Harris and Severn Darden under the direction of Paul Sills, Barbara played the intellectual teenage daughter of Severn's academic. At the beginning of the scene, Barbara is in her room, on the phone with a friend, reading a juicy passage from Erich Fromm's book *The Art of Loving*. She is interrupted by a knock on the door. Hanging up, she welcomes Severn into her room. He hasn't talked to her in a few days and wants to know what is going on in her busy life.

Of course he has seen her report card—all As again. "What can I do?" she says, "I'm precocious." He notices she's painted her room white. Yes, she says, she thinks her Matisse prints will look better on these walls, and she treats him to a cup of one of her new enthusiasms, Turkish coffee. With a solicitous tone, she observes how tired he looks. He mentions he's been staying up late, working on a book relating Chinese culture to the rise of the Nazis. "But that's the one they won't publish," she says, her voice full of concern. He acknowledges that it's "a twisty point," but he wants to see it through.

He returns to the subject of her recent activities. She tells of a modern dance class she's been attending. It's based on the idea of "moving bone upward" (whatever that means) to the accompaniment not of music but spoken text. She patiently explains to him how profound this is and tells him he'll have the opportunity to see what she's talking about when she and the other girls in her class perform a recital in front of a fountain in a Chicago park.

But that's still classwork, he says. What about outside of class? Did she have fun visiting the Murphys last weekend? Oh, yes, she insists. The Murphys had a party for the grown-ups. She and the other kids had their own little gathering in the basement. Severn presses her on what happened there, and she says, "Well, it was kind of an experiment." The experiment turns out to have involved marijuana. Severn is upset. He doesn't want his teenage daughter to be a junkie. She tries to explain that a university study says that you can't actually get addicted to grass. He waves her rationalizations aside. It's illegal and it's not a cause worth going to jail for. He wants her to promise she'll never do it again. She promises, putting some energy into her demonstration of sincerity, making faces as she talks about how little she enjoyed smoking dope. "Don't act," he says, "just promise."

She thanks him for helping her purge her guilt. And now, if he doesn't mind, she has other things to do. But he has more questions. What else happened at the Murphys'? Did something perhaps happen with young Fred Stewart? She knows what he's after. "Well, it was an experiment," she says again. "Another experiment?" he responds. "You had a very scientific weekend." Point blank, he asks her if she made love with Fred. She says that's a matter of semantics. No, he replies, it's a matter of mechanics. Did she?

She offers up a new expression of contrition. She'll go live in a convent. "You can't go to a convent," he says. "They won't let you take your horse." As she continues to berate herself, he says, "You have no reason to feel guilty, even though what you did was wrong." He corrects himself. He understands what happened. She and Fred have feelings for each other and they acted on them. No, she says, with an almost pitying tone at the naïveté of his assumption.

And she tries to explain. Has he read this Erich Fromm book? No? Well, in it Fromm puts forward a new theory of love. It's not what the pop songs say—passion at first sight and that sort of thing. No, according to Fromm, love is a craft, acquired and honed by practice. And that's what she and Fred were doing. Investigating Fromm's theories.

Severn insists that surely there must be feeling between them. She says that in the Freudian sense there were "ego needs," and she raises her book to quote from it. But he gently takes the book from her and refers to the image of young love in *Romeo and Juliet*. She dismisses Shakespeare's pair as a pair of neurotics, but he presses on, quoting a poetic passage in which Juliet speaks of Romeo.

Barbara turns away from him, a pained expression on her face. Finishing Juliet's speech, Severn says, "You must have felt something of that for Fred, didn't you?" She shakes her head and says, "Father, he doesn't want me." With a sob, she buries herself in his arms. He tries to comfort and reassure her. "He wants you," he says. "No," she says, tears glistening as she leans against her father's chest and the lights go down.

In this scene, Severn and Barbara are father and daughter. That is their biological relationship. But much of what is arresting about the piece is the variety of ways they can *be* father and daughter.

When she instructs him in the way to cope with Turkish coffee and how to appreciate modern dance, Barbara is playing the cultural adventurer to Severn's fuddy-duddy.

When he speaks of his work on what is clearly a hopeless book, her concern that he not be bruised by disappointment is almost maternal.

As she chatters on about her theories, we see the concern goes both ways. As intellectually sharp as she is, she is still a sixteen-year-old girl at an age where she can be hurt by experimentation and exploration. He is trying to figure out what is the best way to be a father to her. "You have no reason to feel guilty, even though what you did was wrong," succinctly expresses his conflicting impulses. On the one hand, he's not very happy to learn that at such a young age she has lost her virginity. On the other, her heart has been broken. The authoritarian impulse is overwhelmed by the empathetic one.

I believe that scenes and plays have a natural drift to the truth. The final image of Barbara, in tears as she is comforted by Severn, expresses the final truth of this scene: under her initial pose as a would-be sophisticate and his as a distracted academic—and indeed under all the other poses, roles, and voices they use with each other—the essence of the relationship is of a sensitive child needing the comfort and protection of a loving father.

I explained in the previous lesson how works can be based on a character torn between responsibilities and relationships with two or more other characters. "First Affair" demonstrates that a character may use a variety of voices in conversation with another *single* character, which suggests that a script may be based on the conflicting roles within a relationship between two characters.

Another example: Jean Anouilh's *Becket* concerns how King Henry II and Becket start as best friends and become antagonists. Henry is irked that the sacred power of the Church challenges his secular power, and, over Becket's objection, he conceives the idea to nominate his partner in mischief as Archbishop of Canterbury. Henry assumes that Becket's primary loyalty will remain with him, but Becket finds his calling as Archbishop and becomes a champion of the Church against Henry's authority. In his rage and betrayal, Henry cries out, "Will no one rid me of this meddlesome priest?" Some of his followers see this as license to murder Becket at his duties, and Henry ends up having to do penance for his moral complicity in the bloody deed.

This story would not pack the power it does were it not for the fastness of the friendship between the two men at the beginning of the story. Becket's devotion to Henry at the start prefigures the depth of his subsequent devotion to God. A profligate is transformed into a martyr. The conclusion of the play presents the final reckoning between the two men, dramatically defining the difference in their characters.

Klute, the Alan J. Pakula suspense film from a screenplay by Andy and Dave Lewis, contains a virtuoso scene early in the picture in which Jane Fonda's character (Bree) trots out a series of voices in her confrontation with the character played by Donald Sutherland (Klute).

Here's the setup: John Klute's friend Tom has disappeared. Klute, a small-town cop, has taken a leave of absence to go to New York and pursue the only lead he has to Tom's disappearance—a call girl named Bree who may have had a date with him and might be receiving bizarre letters from him. Bree is not interested in being helpful, but Klute isn't easily discouraged. He taps her phone, and, one night, he follows her to the garment district where he watches her strip while reciting an erotic fantasy for an old man. When she returns from this date, he confronts her with the evidence of her activities. The implication: if she doesn't help him, he'll see to it that she gets nailed for violating her parole. She reluctantly agrees to cooperate. They go to her apartment.

They both are pursuing their objectives. He wants information. She wants the incriminating tapes.

She begins by playing halfhearted hostess, offering him a beer he doesn't want (and, it turns out, she doesn't have in her fridge anyway). Trying to project an image of reasonableness under pressure, she tells him she cooperated with the New York police in their hunt for Tom. When he shows her a photo of Tom, she cynically cracks, "Family-type man—figures." She describes her old life as a Park Avenue call girl, representing it as a life of glamour and privilege. Then, with a shudder, she goes on to tell him she has received bizarre letters that she thought might be from a customer who abused her physically, letters that the police thought were from Tom. However, nothing conclusive came from the police investigation. Her recitation is interrupted by a phone call from a prospective client, and we hear a little of her playfully seductive, "professional" voice. Cutting short the call, she turns back to Klute. He asks about her relationship to her former pimp, and she dismisses his understanding of this as the impressions of a "square." When Klute asks how the date with the old man tonight was set up, she flares with moral outrage. "You saw that? Goddamn you!" And then she attacks Klute as a hypocrite, suggesting his seeming morality may be a front for a secret "bag" of his own. Putting the brakes on her anger and believing she has told him all she can, she begins to disrobe, suggesting the exchange of "a party" for the tapes. He asks her not to undress and she remarks, in a cheerfully satiric tone, "Men have paid $200 for me and here you are turning down a freebie. You could get a perfectly good dishwasher for that." He approaches her and leads her to the bed. She thinks she's succeeded in her seduction and begins to grope him, but as he sits her down on the bed he tells her he's heard sounds that suggest that someone is on her roof. He draws his pistol and goes in pursuit, and the final image of the scene is of her sitting in terror.

I can only suggest the complexity of this scene, which is built on the contrast between the steady professional, undistractable attitude that Klute maintains and the barrage of different tones and poses that Bree unleashes. She moves from one voice to another, and one role to another, with a speed that dazzles. The film is largely about the war between these various roles and about her battle to find a persona that will not only help her survive but make the transition to a healthy woman capable of sustaining a sharing relationship.

In *With and Without*, I wrote an extended scene based on this principle.

At this point in the play, Jill, trying to cope with what she believes is the end of her marriage, has brought back to the summer house a local named Glen she has picked up at a bar in town. It is night. They stand on a deck overlooking a lake, drinking wine. The sight of neighbors frolicking prompts Glen to remember a skinny-dipping episode in a pool with some young women in Los Angeles when he was young. Because he took his glasses off to get into the pool, he couldn't see much.

JILL: You even remember her name?

GLEN: Whose name?

JILL: Whoever she was you ended up with.

GLEN: No, that didn't happen.

JILL: No? All that potential for nookie and nothing? That's all there is to the story? Just that you paddled around bare-assed in the same pool with some women you couldn't see very well? . . . . . That's what you call a good time?

Here, Jill's voice is light and bantering, tossing around jokey sexual references ("nookie," "bare-assed") without inhibition. Rather than matching her tone, he tries to maintain a thoughtful, more philosophical voice.

GLEN: Actually, there was something nice about being able to all be naked together without feeling the necessity of taking it further. It's like a truce had been declared.

JILL: A truce? From what?

GLEN: The usual will-we-won't-we stuff. Not that anybody said anything like that. Made an announcement or anything. Just there was a sort of understanding.

JILL: A sex-free zone?

GLEN: Hunh?

JILL: Like a nuclear-free zone, a sex-free zone.

GLEN: Like that, yeah. No pressure. No expectations. We all felt safe. Like we were all observing, well, like I said—a flag of truce.

His philosophical tone is catchy. She switches from the wisecracks to a more serious, rueful tone:

JILL: I'd like to know where to get one of those.

GLEN: A flag of truce?

JILL: Sometimes to be able to call a time out. To be able to say, "Hey, could we, for a little while, put all this crap aside?"

Later in the scene, she learns that he's a carpenter who makes decks not unlike the one they're on at the moment.

JILL: I work with carpenters sometimes.

GLEN: Really how?

JILL: If I need something built for a function.

GLEN: A function? What do you—

JILL: I'm a partner at Iris Broder Promotions.

GLEN: And that is—?

JILL: Events planning.

GLEN: And that is—?

JILL: Say you've got a daughter getting married and five, six hundred grand to do it up right.

GLEN: Five, six hundred grand?

JILL: Hey, I know one topped a million two.

GLEN: So you do what?

JILL: Conceptualize, organize, schedule. If we're doing something on a gypsy theme, maybe I'll fly violinists in from Budapest. Or if I need a gazebo to be built in the ballroom at the Plaza, I'll work with designers. Keep an eye on construction.

GLEN: Carpenters.

JILL: And electricians, yeah. Though I don't really deal directly at that level. That's for the person I've brought in to supervise to handle. And then, you know, photographers. . . . . It's like being a producer.

GLEN: A lot of people work on these things, hunh?

JILL: For the big projects, it can go north of a hundred.

Here we're offered a sample of Jill's professional voice—the one that represents herself as being able to deal with large-budget, high-profile events without breaking into a sweat. She's also signaling to Glen that she lives on, well, a higher social plane than he does. He decides to push her to state this more explicitly.

GLEN: And you're the boss.

JILL: Oh, I don't know.

GLEN: You said you hire people—

JILL: Some.

GLEN: And you can fire them.

JILL: Yeah.

GLEN (*His case is made*): You're the boss.

JILL: I'm *a* boss.

GLEN: D*o* you fire people?

JILL: I try to hire the right people to begin with so I don't have to.

GLEN: But you *have* fired people?

JILL: Part of the job.

GLEN: You set standards, and if people don't meet them—

JILL: First, maybe a warning shot over their head.

GLEN: A touch of the whip?

JILL: Just to get them focused. Mostly it works.

GLEN: But sometimes—
(*He signals, "Out of there."*)

JILL: Part of the job.

GLEN: And if you fire them from one job, you're not likely to hire them for another.

JILL: No.

GLEN: So when you're in the neighborhood, people are on their best behavior.

JILL: Yes, I inspire fear. No, I'm pretty easy to get along with. Long as you do your job.

GLEN: I'll remember that.

He has maneuvered her into conceding the power she has, and in acknowledging that she hires and fires people very much like him. Afraid of scaring him off, she doesn't want to continue to make too big a deal about her higher professional status, so she makes jokes mocking the image of herself as dragon lady.

JILL: Doing this kind of work can spoil you. You make a decision, you tell people the way you want it—

GLEN: They do it.

JILL: But outside of work—People have this annoying tendency to do what *they* want to do.

GLEN: And you can't fire them.

JILL: There are days I'd like to. Like my mother. She'd open an envelope from me, there's this pink slip, maybe a little handwritten note. "Thanks for all your hard work, but we're downsizing the family. Best of luck in your future parenting career."

You probably recognize this as drawing on the professional roles versus personal role dynamic that was discussed in Lesson 5.

Later, Glen talks about coping with a divorce he didn't want and Jill sees him now as someone who has gone through things she may very well be going through soon. It is as though she's the newcomer to the state of divorce, looking to him as a veteran to show her some of the landmarks. In this passage, by virtue of his greater experience, he has higher status.

GLEN: The divorce wasn't my idea.

JILL: Another guy?

GLEN: Mmmmm.

JILL: That must have done wonders for your ego.

GLEN: Made me stand real tall in my son's eyes. Thirteen years old—you have all of these semi-adult impulses and appetites, but you don't have the power to do anything about them. So you look around for someone to identify with who's got muscle.

JILL: Sylvester Stallone, Spiderman, Arnold.

GLEN: You sure don't look at a dad who couldn't hold the family together. That's the first job of a dad, and he thinks I blew it. . . . . You read about how kids take after their parents? For his sake I hope not.

Jill realizes that if Glen lapses into moodiness and self-pity, she isn't likely to get the kind of company she wants from him tonight. So she makes a conscious decision to shift the tone. She fetches a boom box playing romantic dance music and begins to make moves on him. She reestablishes a playful, seductive tone. Things seem to be going well when he says—

GLEN: I should tell you something.

JILL: What?

GLEN: I really haven't been with anybody else since my wife and I broke up. The divorce.

JILL: Me neither.

GLEN: Oh, well then you understand.

JILL: We can take it real easy, if that's what you want.

GLEN: It's not that I'm made out of china.

JILL: No, I do understand. But while we're talking, if there's something you used to do with her—with your wife—in bed, you know?

GLEN: Like what?

JILL: Oh, scratch her head or something—like a habit thing—if you could do me the favor of not doing that with me.

GLEN: OK.

JILL: Tonight's going to be whatever it's going to be, but I would like it if it's me you're with, not that I'm a stand-in. Or a lie-in.

GLEN: You got it.

JILL: All right then.

GLEN: Shall my lawyer call your lawyer, draw up the contract?

Glen's joke here is based on the shift in voices he's noticed arising between the two of them—from seduction to something approaching a contractual agreement.

JILL: Hunh?

GLEN: A joke.

JILL: I don't understand it.

GLEN: We've just gone through this negotiation.

JILL (*Laughs*): Oh. Yes.

GLEN: I mean, we've basically decided what we're going to do and we haven't even touched each other.

JILL: We should get around to that.

GLEN: Break the ice a little.

JILL: Every journey begins with one step.

(A *beat. Glen goes to her and kisses her.*)

GLEN: Hello.

JILL: Hello.

GLEN: This could work.

JILL: For tonight anyway.

The configuration is simple—two people talking. What makes it possible for the scene to run nearly twenty-five minutes and hold the stage is that, even though only two people are talking, they present to each other and encounter from each other a dozen or so different aspects of their personalities—wistful, confrontational, worldly, unsophisticated, cynical, idealistic, satiric, corny, angry, apologetic, conspiratorial, professional, bawdy, tender, legalistic, seductive, inhibited, romantic, practical. This kind of scene is simultaneously one of the more difficult kinds to write and one of the most rewarding to see good actors sink their teeth into, showing the various and contrasting colors of the characters they're playing.

To restate something I mentioned in passing above, this scene and others built similarly conclude when the characters work their way through various aspects (or masks) till their truest aspects emerge—at least their truest voices in this particular encounter. In the scene between Barbara and Severn, their truest aspects are a vulnerable daughter and a caring father. In the scene between Bree and Klute, their truest aspects are a terrified woman and her determined protector. In the scene between Jill and Glen, their truest aspects are a woman looking for temporary intimacy and a lonely man hoping for more.

Incidentally, what I said in the previous lesson about different costuming representing different roles with different people applies to different roles with the same person. In scene two of *Streetcar*, after Blanche has unsuccessfully attempted to charm her brother-in-law, Stanley compels her to get down to the business of explaining what has become of the family's assets. Donning glasses to look through the legal papers in her trunk chronicling the loss of Belle Reve, she transforms from a flirt to a clerk.

> **Assignment Eight:** Write a scene between two people in which at least one of the people assumes different voices with the other.

By Matt Mezzacappa

> *(A theatre lobby. A teenage boy and girl—Joey and Kelly— are rehearsing a scene.)*

JOEY: "You are more beautiful than a rose picked by a princess."

KELLY: "But the princess is far lovelier than I."

JOEY: "No lady could surpass you but a goddess."

KELLY: "Forever, then, beneath one, till I die."[1]

JOEY *(Moving closer to her)*: "Yet, if you kissed me, heaven would descend."

KELLY: "Then do not in—"

> *(She stops.)*

JOEY *(Prompting)*: "Then do not in cruel doubt's hand me suspend"!

KELLY: Okay. Sorry.[2]

JOEY: "Yet, if you kissed me, heaven would descend."

KELLY: "Then do not in cruel doubt's hand me suspend."

> *(Joey moves to kiss her.)*

Wait, when do we sit down on the bench?[3]

JOEY: After we kiss.

KELLY: Are you sure?

JOEY: Yeah. When you say, "Let us now enjoy the falling sun."[4]

KELLY: "Sinking sun."

JOEY: Oh. So, let's go back to—

KELLY: Who goes to the bench first?

JOEY: I think you do, and I say, like, "Why dost thou thy worshiper forsake?"

KELLY: Oh. Oh yeah.

> *(She laughs.)*

She's got you whipped.[5]

JOEY: That would be the point.[6]

KELLY: I know, Joe.

JOEY: OK, so—"If you kissed me heaven would descend."

KELLY: Do you think they want us back there yet?[7]

JOEY: Ummm, no, they'll tell us. So—

KELLY: They're doing the dance scene now?

JOEY: Yeah, but—

KELLY: How long does that take?

JOEY: I don't know. Depends.

KELLY: OK.

JOEY: OK. Let's go back—

KELLY: OK, so I leave you here to go back to the bench.[8]

JOEY: Wait. We should go back before that.

KELLY: Joey, I don't—

JOEY: How are we going to do the scene in the play if we don't do it in rehearsal?[9]

KELLY: OK.[10]

JOEY: "Yet if you kissed me heaven would descend."

> *(Kelly takes a deep breath, then—)*

KELLY: "Then do not in cruel doubt's hand me—suspend."

> *(Joey moves in to kiss her. Kelly tenses and lets Joey kiss her for a second. Her lips are sealed shut.)*

JOEY: Is that how "my goddess" would kiss her lover?

KELLY: Actor doesn't give other actor notes.[11]

JOEY: Actress kisses actor if it is called for in the script.[12]

KELLY: I kissed you, didn't I?[13]

1. The discontinuity between the modern setting and the archaic language instantly sets up the promise that at some point contemporary colloquial speech will break out. The anticipation of this sets up a nice tension.

2. The first confirmation that, yes, these two are not speaking spontaneously but rehearsing.

3. Her question is so neatly timed to interrupt the kiss that we suspect her request for information is disingenuous.

4. His voice here is put on—a "serious actor" voice that is meant to suggest that he's taking her questions seriously.

5. Her voice here is purposely flip and anachronistic (an implied mocking of the attempt at high literary language in the scene being played) and contains a shorthand for a vulgarism that she probably knows is a little jarring coming from a teenage girl.

6. Here he succumbs to the impulse to be sarcastic, probably an indication of his impatience with her.

7. Now her voice is a pretense of concern for the expectations of others in the project.

8. Now she affects a matter-of-fact, pseudo-professional tone, which is meant to camouflage her reluctance to practice the kiss.

9. A determined quality has replaced the hesitation of a few lines before.

10. A touch of resignation as she realizes she's probably stuck.

11. The clipped phrasing of this line suggests she is quoting an abbreviated version of a rule.

12. His reply is a sarcastic echo of her line, further evidence of his impatience.

13. This is the most "teenage" of her lines. The fact that it comes at the end of the scene suggests that this is her true voice in this situation, the one that most accurately reflects her real feelings.

The scene plays with a number of voices—the fictional voices of the characters they are playing, the voices of the people they are pretending to be to each other (something that might pass for adult or professional-ish), and their real teenage voices. The fun of this piece arises from juxtaposing and contrasting them.

By Stephen Tesher

> *(Linda sits on the couch watching television. Peter enters.)*

LINDA: So . . . ?

PETER: Hi, honey, I'm ho-ome.[1]

LINDA: Is she blonde? Brunette? Exotic? Which?[2]

PETER: I don't—what's today—Wednesday?[3]

LINDA: Thursday.

PETER: Thursday. That's the redhead.

LINDA: What about a secretary?

PETER: Oh no. Never in-house.

LINDA: How about that take-out?[4]

PETER: Take-out?

LINDA: Yeah. Chinese.

PETER: A Chinese—are you kidding me?

LINDA: No, I'm not kidding. I'm hungry![5]

PETER: Oh, take-out![6] Okay. You mean order in.

LINDA: Same thing.

PETER: Not always.[7]

LINDA: I expect you home by eight, it's past eleven—[8]

PETER: I know, I know. I was done with my work—[9]

LINDA *(Bringing him menus)*: Honey? Food first?
> *(All business.)*

Chinese, Thai, Mexican . . . ?[10]

PETER: Mexican.

LINDA: Chinese.

> *(She shoves the menu at him, puts the rest away.)*

So, you're out the door . . .[11]

PETER: Yes! Out the door, they dump a pile of last-minute bullshit—

LINDA: They dump it on your phone?[12]

PETER: Hey, I have to put the redhead somewhere.[13]

LINDA: I want the steamed dumplings. Spinach. Steamed.[14]

PETER: I'm calling?

LINDA: And a Diet Coke.

　　(*Beat.*)

Can she help you?[15]

PETER: She's a partner's wife.[16]

LINDA: Mendelson?

PETER: Sterling.

LINDA: Sterling? That pig?

PETER: I hear he cheats on his wife.

　　(*Beat.*)

Let me go wash up.

LINDA: Hug first.[17]

PETER: Honey, I've been sweating over briefs and reports, subway traffic—

LINDA: You are joking about the redhead aren't you?[18]

PETER (*Moving to her*): Baby, of course I am.

　　(*She smiles, leans into him. He backs away with—*)

Now let me wash up.

LINDA: Hugs![19]

　　(*She jumps onto his arms and holds on tight.*)

PETER (*Trying to shake her*): Don't you want me to order . . . ?[20]

LINDA (*Sniffing*): What's that smell?

PETER: Look Linda, I come home from a long day of work, I want to let off a little steam. The perfume's from the subway. Theatre crowd. The whole car stank.

LINDA: They smoke cigarettes on the subway, too?

PETER: What?

LINDA: You're supposed to be quitting.

PETER: I am. No—Feldman stops me—we take a couple of beers at Jeremy's. Lots of smoke—

LINDA: And perfume.

PETER: Right.

LINDA: You calling the place or am I?

PETER (*Handing her phone*): It's this city. One day I'll come home smelling like fish . . . or salami . . . or . . .

LINDA: Redheads?

    (*Beat.*)

Why would you think I'd smell perfume? I smell cigarettes, not perfume. You know I hate the smoke but you're more worried about the perfume . . .

PETER: I'm not worried, I'm—look, you want to call Sherry? She was there, too.

LINDA: Who's Sherry?

PETER: Feldman's intern. She can corroborate this whole story.

LINDA: You feel the need for corroboration?

PETER: I feel the need for some fresh air, actually. It's getting a little dense in here.

LINDA: Going to Sherry's?

PETER: I'm thinking the Holiday Inn.

LINDA: Alone?

    (*Pause.*)

PETER: You want to come with?

    (*Linda nods "yes." Peter pulls her into his arms.*)

PETER: We'll bring the menus.

    (*She nods again.*)

Now I'm going to wash up.

    (*Peter heads into the bathroom. Linda moves to the coatrack, smells Peter's coat. She starts to cry out but holds it back.*)

PETER (*From bathroom*): How about a bottle of wine?

LINDA: Sure.

    (*She doesn't move.*)

1. He starts with an invitation to play (and mock) stereotyped roles of working husband returning to waiting wife.

2. She affects a "sophisticated" role—the wife too hip to care about a husband's supposed dalliances.

3. His voice now matches hers, signaling a temporary agreement to play.

4. Dropping the play to deal with a real immediate question.

5. She's signaling to him that he failed to follow her lead into the realm of the real and practical. One gets the sense that she's confused him on purpose.

6. Playing catch-up.

7. I read this as his attempt at playfulness.

8. And I read this as her refusal to match his voice and play along.

9. He's shooting for a mixture of apology and seeming candor.

10. And again, she switches on him.

11. And again, she switches. She's clearly signalling that she has control of the agenda here.

12. Sarcasm.

13. A strained attempt to bring back the joking.

14. Back to the practical business voice again.

15. She shifts tone again, back to a playfully cynical attitude.

16. He's playing catch-up again.

17. This could be played different ways—as an imperative or as an open request for reassurance.

18. The most overt and least-guarded expression of her real concern.

19. "Hugs" sounds almost adolescent, a little desperately cute.

20. To my eye, this reads as an evasion fueled by his embarrassment.

I'm not going to go on line by line, but the scene shifts between a variety of voices for each of the characters—willfully playful, investigative (like a lawyer or detective), accusatory, conciliatory, indignant, weary, seductive, and finally, as she begins to settle on what she believes is the truth and that she is unwilling to risk what an open confrontation might bring, resigned.

SIDEBAR 3

Stage Directions

"I CROSS THEM OUT."

This has become something of a mantra for actors regarding stage directions.

I understand the impulse. Some writers reach for a parenthetical on every line.

NORA (*Coyly*): Well, what do you want to do tonight?

IRA (*Wryly*): As if I really have anything to say about it.

NORA (*With irritation*): Excuse me?

IRA (*Trying to make peace*): Never mind.

NORA (*Insistently*): No, if you have something to say—

IRA (*Interrupting*): Say, isn't that the Loch Ness monster?

NORA (*Undistracted*): That won't work.

IRA (*Seductively*): Is that a new perfume?

When instructions precede every utterance, I don't blame actors for reacting (*petulantly*). Interpretive instructions laid on so thick signal mistrust. Actors read this as the writer saying, "I don't think you know your job."

Actually, what it may mean is that the *writer* doesn't know the actor's job. The more experience you have working with first-rate players, the more you realize that they don't need you to coach them phrase by phrase on the tone of a line or what you intended writing it. They come to rehearsal to discover—under the guidance of the director and in the company of their colleagues—what behavior (including gesture, intonation, and inflection) needs to be created in order to support the text.

Directors, too, are less than cheerful about too much specific advice from the author.

Rachel enters DSL and crosses to the window USC. She lets out a gasp and runs to the painting on the wall SR. She hesitates for three seconds before removing the painting and revealing the safe behind it. As she dials the combination, Brad enters through the door USL, his figure backlit by the glow of the sunset behind him. Hearing him, Rachel spins around and her hand flies to her mouth in a gesture of fear.

Yes, there are descriptions of this ilk in some published scripts. Mostly old scripts.

Some years ago, it was common practice for the publisher of an acting edition to base it on the script created by the stage manager of the original (usually Broadway) production. This production script would include diagrams and detailed notations as to where the cast moved, what they did when, and so forth. (Stage managers still make such scripts—especially if part of their responsibilities is to rehearse understudies.) But as I say, in days gone by, these notes were also integrated into the published editions. The thinking was that those putting up amateur and educational productions could use all the help they could get. A typical acting edition often also contained a ground plan of the original set, specifying the locations of the doors and windows and fireplace and such. So, if the Burbary Community Theatre's designer built a set for *Maureen's Big Night* consistent with the ground plan in the Samuel French book, and if the director followed the published instructions to push the actors around SL and USR and so forth, Burbary would see a vague approximation of how the show moved when Helen Hayes played Maureen's mother back in 1952.

But—just to pound the point home—these blocking notations were not written by the playwright. Robert Anderson did not put instructions of this sort in the manuscript of *Tea and Sympathy*. He trusted that his director, Elia Kazan, was perfectly capable of helping the cast find appropriate and motivated places to move without such detailed marching orders. And, if Anderson had presumed to be so specific in his text, Kazan would have ignored these notations.

These days, playwrights tend to put only what is required by way of descriptive matter in their scripts—essential elements of the set, essential props, essential actions. And, mostly, the published editions of these scripts do not reflect specific staging ideas created by the director.

There are a couple of reasons for this. For one thing, these days straight plays are rarely sent out on tours copying the original Broadway staging. Rather, because of the explosion of regional theatres since the mid-1960s, managements located in various cities put up their own distinct, individual versions. The production of Paula Vogel's *How I Learned to Drive* in Chicago may be every bit as good as the production in Santa Fe, but the sets will look different and the directors will have arrived at different solutions to the problems Vogel poses in her text. Since writers know that a successful play is going to receive many distinct professional productions (probably in venues of varying sizes and configurations), there is no point in specifying anything more than the information strictly necessary.

Also, directors are getting more possessive about their contributions. The legal issues relating to who owns the blocking a director creates on a signature production haven't been definitively hashed out, but among many dramatists the moral imperative is clear: don't put any staging invented by the director into your script unless the director has given you permission to do so. In some instances, playwrights have actively defended their directors' claims to rights. In a key case, Terrence McNally supported Joe Mantello when Mantello successfully pursued a Florida company that had appropriated without permission elements specific to Mantello's original staging of *Love! Valour! Compassion!* in New York.

Besides, if one is lucky enough to write a play that is given a number of productions, part of the fun of being a writer is to see how these productions differ. Every time your work is staged freshly, it gives you a chance to experience it anew and find different values and aspects in it.

I'm not saying that you should write no stage directions at all. Clearly it is important to establish the environment in which the action is to take place, and a word or two about the impressions the characters make onstage can be useful (for instance, their ages are often relevant). And certainly you need to mention if Captain Aldershot pulls out a pistol.

But stage directions tend to be taken seriously in inverse proportion to the number of them you include. If you offer interpretive assistance on virtually every line (as in the dialogue between Nora and Ira above), the actors will quickly pull out black felt-tip pens and obliterate them. On the other hand, if there is only the occasional bit of advice (once every few pages, perhaps), this is likely to be heeded.

Rather than pummelling the actors with a barrage of adverbs, I tend to put what advice I want to offer into the form of an essay that is published at the back of my scripts.

For instance, here's the advice I offer the actor playing Ted in *Flyovers*:

"Ted should not be played as an overt bully. If the actor will simply pursue the objectives of appearing to be an ingratiating host and trying to win Oliver's respect for his ideas, then the rest will fall into place. The menace does not have to be underlined. Also, Ted's objective in the scene with Lianne is to protect her from embarrassing herself. He is in love with her, and her distress causes him great pain."

I say nothing here about the interpretation of specific moments. Most of what I offer is by way of identifying Ted's objectives. I trust that if the actor truthfully pursues Ted's objectives, whatever specific behavior he comes up with will be consistent with my intentions. And, if I'm lucky, he will surprise me by coming up with stuff I haven't already imagined.

Finally, I point out that Shakespeare's texts are published with the names of the characters, succinct identifications of each scene's setting, necessary entrances and exits, and such props as come into play. The paucity of stage directions doesn't seem to have undermined the attractiveness of his scripts.

9
LESSON
Of Context and Conversation

A CONFESSION: I'VE BEEN TRYING TO TRICK YOU.

As I've gone over the principles of negotiation and different voices and made assignments based on these principles, I have been trying to get you to do something that is among the most difficult technical challenges facing dramatic writers: write high-context exposition.

OK, this word "exposition" sounds familiar. That's the stuff—the given circumstances—that the audience needs to learn in order to understand the action of the story. What does the phrase "high-context" mean? And why does it belong next to "exposition"?

As I wrote in *The Dramatist's Toolkit*, anthropologist Edward T. Hall's work deals with how we transmit information to each other through message systems other than the literal meanings of the words we exchange. In his books *The Silent Language*, *The Hidden Dimension*, *Beyond Culture*, and *The Dance of Time*, he examines the roles that body language, inflection, architecture, interior design, defensible space, sequence, pace, and synchronicity play in interpersonal communication. (I am summarizing to the point of absurdity; Hall deserves to be studied firsthand.) He introduced the terms "high context" and "low context" in *Beyond Culture*.

People who have a low-context relationship (and who speak low-context dialogue) are those who are not familiar with each other and so must explain themselves. We frequently find ourselves in low-context relationships with experts—doctors, lawyers, accountants, plumbers. These are people who reign over systems of knowledge and lexicons connected to them made up of terms that are mostly alien to our ears. We rely on these experts to explain to us what a left-handed gasket, deficit financing, and torts are and how such things relate to our particular problems. Experts are the possessors and translators of arcane information, and part of their function is rooted in the disparity between what they know and what we know. Where there is a disparity of knowledge or information between people, you have a low-context relationship.

A low-context relationship can occur outside of a professional encounter, of course. As I write this, I'm on a train traveling to Chicago. Over breakfast in the dining car, I had a conversation with a young man from Amsterdam who is making a round-the-world trip. I had not met him before. He introduced himself and described his itinerary, and, in turn, I told him a little about my reason for being on this train. Because we did not know each other before and preferred not to eat in silence, we chose to share information about ourselves. We had reason to indulge in low-context exposition.

At the beginning of a play or film, the audience is in a low-context relationship with the characters and the world being presented. And so the writer may have the impulse to explain what the characters have done before and detail the events prior to the beginning of the story's action.

This is easier to do when the characters who are carrying the action begin in a low-context situation themselves. At the beginning of *Streetcar*, Blanche is new to the world of New Orleans and to Stanley and Mitch, so there is cause for her to explain things to both of them. Under pressure from Stanley, she details how Belle Reve was lost. To Mitch, she tells of her marriage and her part in the suicide of her young husband. At no point does the material sound as if it has been written primarily to inform us; Williams has established that she has good reason to tell these things to these men, so Blanche's articulation of this material about her past doesn't seem forced. And during the course of these scenes, we learn what we need to. The fact that she is a newcomer to this world (as are we) gives us the opportunity to learn as she learns about the ways of the French Quarter.

To state what is probably obvious, the dialogue appropriate for people who don't know each other well or who aren't privy to the same information or knowledge is low-context dialogue.

But I doubt you will want the leading figures in every script you write to be strangers to each other at the beginning. It's hard to write, say, a family play and justify having Mom and Dad explain to each other things like how many children they have or that Grandma died in the winter of '78. People who have such shared experiences and information speak *assuming* that these things are known and so don't need to be articulated. They speak in a shorthand. They have a high-context relationship, so they speak high-context dialogue.

But here's the problem: your characters may know this stuff, but your audience doesn't. And your audience needs to know much of this in order to follow the action of the play.

Some writers have been tempted to have these characters explain this material to each other anyway. The result? They force characters in high-context relationships to speak low-context dialogue. Mom and Dad tell each other how many children they have and what their names are. And it sounds phony. The audience can tell that the only reason these people are talking about these matters is so that the writer can transmit the information to people in the dark overhearing the conversation, but in so doing the characters' credibility has been undermined.

So, if you can't have characters talk about what you want the audience to know, how do you do this? How do you *do* high-context exposition?

This takes us back to material I introduced at the beginning of these lessons: the power of the unspoken word. You don't have to *tell* the audience the circumstances. In fact, you run the risk of undermining the effectiveness of the material if you have it articulated. Instead, you present behavior that leads the audience to think, "Ah, they wouldn't be doing this, if *that* circumstance didn't pertain." We're back to the idea of premises-and-conclusions. Again, we're offering the audience data and inviting them to infer from this data.

This is part of what I was after in taking you through the assignments in which characters negotiated over objects. Look again at the scene I included at the end of Lesson 2 on page 27—the one between Mark Benzo and Tina. See how much we are able to figure out about their relationship through the way he putters around her bathroom? At no point does either of them say that this is a relatively new relationship, and at no point does either of them say that he is cheating on another partner, yet these are conclusions at which a reasonably awake viewer must arrive. Just as in Assignment 1 in response to which I had you make the audience conjure up the unspoken word, so the challenge here is to encourage the audience to conjure up the exposition themselves.

One way is to have the characters deal with a problem that could exist only given the circumstance you wish to expose. You don't have them talk about the circumstance itself, you have them negotiate over the problem.

Let me give you a modest example:

(*Mae is washing dishes, Joe is drying them.*)

MAE: Oh damn.

JOE: What?

MAE: This one's cracked.

JOE: Well, you can get another one, can't you?

MAE: Get another?

JOE: You're going to the movies on Saturday, aren't you?

MAE: But that'll be a different pattern. They were handing out this pattern last summer when they were showing that serial about the Mole People.

JOE: A dish is a dish, isn't it?

MAE: But you want them to match. All these have bluebells on them. What they're giving out now have daisies.

JOE: Can't mix daisies and bluebells?

MAE: It's the point of having a pattern—stuff matches.

JOE: You could say it's a bouquet.

MAE: Very funny. You don't care what impression anything makes. But it reflects on me. If we have company—

JOE: They'll go tsk-tsk that you're mixing daisies with bluebells.

The scene is ostensibly about Mae's problem of how to deal with a damaged set of dishes, but, if I've done this right, this sequence should establish that Mae and Joe are married and that the action takes place during the Depression (as that's when people collected dinner sets piece by piece at their local movie theaters). The scene should also suggest some difference in Mae and Joe's values. Mae likes things just so. Joe doesn't mind if things slide along a little.

> **Assignment Nine:** Create a scene between two people that is high-context. There is a piece of information or backstory or existing circumstance between these two people that you want to get across to the audience, but you *must not* explicitly articulate it. Instead, you create a negotiation that makes the audience think, "Oh, they wouldn't be dealing with this problem if that circumstance didn't pertain."

Advice: Study the opening scene between George and Martha in Edward Albee's *Who's Afraid of Virginia Woolf?* and the first scene between Levine and Williamson in David Mamet's *Glengarry Glen Ross*. Both of them contain beautifully composed high-context exposition.

By *Michael Johnson-Chase*

(*The living room of a house in winter. It is late afternoon. Bernie is fixing a TV. Doorbell rings. Bernie looks up, decides to ignore it. Doorbell rings again.*)

JOSH (*Offstage*): It's me. The door's locked.

BERNIE: How can it be locked?

JOSH: I don't know. It's locked, that's all.

(*Bernie extracts himself from TV, goes to door, opens it, studies the lock. Josh enters.*)

BERNIE: It's self-locking.

JOSH: Oh.

BERNIE: Why didn't you fix it so you could get back in?

JOSH: Well, I didn't . . . because I was thinking about the—[1]

BERNIE: Did you find it? [2]

JOSH: No.

BERNIE: You look in the far back?

JOSH: Went through every box.

BERNIE: Coulda sworn we had one.

JOSH: We did earlier. . . . We used it.

BERNIE: When? Today?

JOSH: That place before lunch. You know, with that . . . the picture of the big church . . .

BERNIE: The Mormons?

JOSH: Yea. Them.

BERNIE: That was the last one?

JOSH: Yea.

BERNIE: I didn't know that. You shoulda told me.

JOSH: Why?

BERNIE: I woulda got one.[3] After lunch. Before the Tazwells.

JOSH: Why?

BERNIE: Insurance.

JOSH: For the Tazwells?

BERNIE: Exactly.

JOSH: They didn't need one.

BERNIE: I know that now. I didn't know that then.

JOSH: When?

BERNIE: Before we went there.

JOSH: Well. All right.

BERNIE: So. . . .You gotta make a run.

JOSH: Now? Well . . . it's ten till.

BERNIE: You got twenty five minutes.[4]

JOSH: It's rush hour. What if I get stuck? I gotta meet Annie at the social worker's at half past. She's coming to talk about—

BERNIE: Ted.

JOSH: Yea.

BERNIE: You told me already.[5]

JOSH: How come you remember that?

BERNIE: You ever listen to what you talk about?

JOSH: Yea.

BERNIE: Then you know why.

JOSH: Know why what? You forgot we needed a coupler.

BERNIE: Jesus.

JOSH: Look, I gotta be there.

BERNIE: OK, fine. Don't get your underwear in a knot.[6]

JOSH: But she's gonna be—

BERNIE: Sure she is. OK? I'll do this without a coupler.

JOSH: How?

BERNIE: Little trick.

JOSH: Stripping the wires? You know what they say at system—

BERNIE: Screw 'em. We both wanna get outta here.

JOSH: But Mrs. Friedman is so nice.

BERNIE: Yes, she's nice. And she's not here right now and she won't care, OK?

JOSH: OK. But you gotta tape it really good.

BERNIE: Of course. Hand me the cutters.

JOSH: Here.

BERNIE: One little moment and then—
 (The TV pops and sizzles.)
What the hell? . . . Oh, man.[7]

JOSH: What?

BERNIE: The power supply was on! Why didn't you unplug it?[8]

JOSH: You told me to get the coupler . . .

BERNIE: I told you to unplug the tube first!

JOSH: I thought you wanted me to get the coupler first.

BERNIE: Goddamn it, Josh.

JOSH: Well, I can't do everything at once. Sorry. So what do we do?

BERNIE: Fix the damn power supply.

JOSH: How?

BERNIE: I don't know. Replace it, I guess.

JOSH: There's nothing to replace it with.

BERNIE: Don't be so negative.

    (Pause.)

JOSH: You're being sarcastic, right? 'Cause we don't have any power supplies in the truck.[9]

BERNIE: Yea, we do.

JOSH: No, we don't.

BERNIE: Wanna bet?

JOSH: Well, I don't—

BERNIE: Where we'd just come from?

JOSH: The Tazwells.

BERNIE: And what'd we do?

JOSH: Put their TV in the—You'd do that?

BERNIE: Hey, you're the one with the meeting. Go get it.

JOSH: But it's so big.

BERNIE: You wanna make a run?

JOSH: No. I got a meeting at half past with Annie at the social—

BERNIE: Shut up, Josh.

JOSH: OK.

BERNIE: So go get the Tazwell TV.

JOSH: I'm going.

    (Josh exits.)

BERNIE: Jesus. What a loser.[10]

    (Silence while Bernie finishes taping the coupler. As he reaches for a knife to cut the tape, Bernie stabs his finger.) Ouch! Damn it!

    (Bernie opens toolbox, takes out box of Band-Aids, and tends to his finger. The doorbell rings.) What?

JOSH *(Offstage)*: The door.

BERNIE: Didn't you push the button?[11]

JOSH: Yea.

BERNIE: So what's the problem?

JOSH: Well, I . . . . My hands are full.

(Pause.)

I'm holding the TV.

(Bernie goes to the door and opens it. Josh is revealed in the doorway holding a TV wider than the door. Pause.)

It's too big.

BERNIE: Turn it sideways.

JOSH: Oh.

(He does and with some effort he manages to enter.)[12]

BERNIE: Put it down.

JOSH: Where?

BERNIE: I don't care. Just put it down.

JOSH: OK.

(Josh looks for the best spot in the room and puts it down. Bernie gets his toolbox and unscrews the back.)

Don't you think that, uh, well—

BERNIE: What?

JOSH: . . . The Tazwells might get upset? Or Mrs. Friedman? If they knew?

BERNIE: They'll never know.

JOSH: I would know. If I was them.

BERNIE: You check your TV power supply often?

JOSH: No.

BERNIE: Then how would you know, Josh?

JOSH: I would look. I mean, if it went to the shop—

BERNIE: No, you wouldn't.

JOSH: Yea, I think I would.

BERNIE: Why?

JOSH: 'Cause . . . Well, someone might do what you're doing.

BERNIE: What we're doing. You would think, maybe somebody switched my power supply? And you would care about this?

JOSH: Yea.

BERNIE: Why would you care?

JOSH: Well, it just wouldn't be mine. It would be somebody else's. I mean, that's not right.

BERNIE: OK, it's not right. But does it matter?

JOSH: Does it matter?

BERNIE: Yea. Really. In the scope of things in the world. For example, does it matter as much as you missing your meeting with that social worker and Annie and Ted?

JOSH: No. Well, maybe. I mean, what about trust?

BERNIE: Trust?

JOSH: Yea, trust that people just do what they're supposed to—

BERNIE: Shut up, Josh.

JOSH: OK.

> *(Pause.)*

Well, I wouldn't trust you.

BERNIE: You wouldn't trust me? You mean you don't trust me?

JOSH: No, I trust you. But I wouldn't trust you if I was your customer.

BERNIE: If you were my customer?

JOSH: Well. Yea. No. I mean, not after this. I mean, now I know you do—we do—

BERNIE: Do what? I'm getting you to your meeting on time, asshole. I'm doing this for you. OK? This is for you.

JOSH: Well, yea. Maybe I shoulda made a run.

> *(Bernie lifts out the power supply.)*

BERNIE: Maybe you should take this and go over there.

> *(Josh takes the power supply over to the other TV, while Bernie gets up.)*

JOSH: You know, I think that Annie could handle—

BERNIE: Gimme the power supply.

> *(Josh hands him the power supply.)*

Thank you.

> *(Bernie begins installing it in the other TV. Pause.)*

What time is it?

JOSH: It's, uh, ten after.

BERNIE: You'll just make it. Pick up the tools.

JOSH: OK.

(*He busies himself with the tools.*)

Did you fix the wires? Where the coupler should be?

BERNIE: Yep. Who ever invented those couplers anyway? Totally unnecessary.

JOSH: Whattaya think about those Mormon guys?[13]

BERNIE: Huh?

JOSH: Well, they must be moral.

BERNIE: Oh yea.

JOSH: What would they think? About us?

BERNIE: They'll never know, will they, Josh?

JOSH: No. I . . . No, guess not.

BERNIE: Poor guys. They'll live forever thinking the world is a kind and gentle place. But we know better, don't we?

JOSH: You're being sarcastic again, right?

BERNIE (*Ready to go*): Voila! Let's go. Don't forget the Tazwell TV. You'll just make your meeting.

(*Josh picks up TV. Bernie opens door. Josh turns sideways.*)

JOSH: Thanks, Bernie.

(*Josh squeezes out with the TV. Bernie picks up his toolbox, glances around, and exits.*)

1. Much of the time you don't need the word "because" in a scene. "Because" explains the relationship between things. In line with my preference for the implicit, I find that often the explanation is not necessary. Just the fact that one line follows another frequently implies causality. So, this line, "Well, I didn't . . . because I was think-ing about the—" lands better on my ear as, "Well, I didn't . . . I was thinking about the—." The audience will supply "because" in their minds. A very small application of the premises-and-conclusions the-ory, but I'm all for cutting any unnecessary words.

2. I like that their conversation is so high-context Bernie knows what Josh is referring to without the use of a specific identifying noun.

3. Here you indeed use the technique I mention above. "I woulda got one" in reaction to "Why?" is more colloquial than, "Because I woulda got one."

4. Good negotiation over plans. I get a strong sense of who has what kind of status through the way Bernie orders Josh around. In the next lesson, I'll go into detail about this technique.

5. "You told me already" is a little lame to me. In the situation of Character A already knowing what Character B is going to say (and being a little impatient about being told something yet again), I frequently have Character A interrupt and say it. So, in this case I might revise like this:

    JOSH: It's rush hour. What if I get stuck? I gotta meet Annie—

    BERNIE (*Interrupting*):—at the social worker's at half past, yes, right.

    From this, the audience can figure out that Bernie's been told this already.

6. This image—"underwear in a twist" is similar to one in an earlier scene—"panties in a knot." Could it be this line and its variations are a little tired now?

7. In upcoming lessons, I'll talk about the usefulness of disruptions. You've arrived at a good example of it on your own.

8. One of the things that particularly impresses me about this scene is—though I know nothing about the technology and have no way of knowing if the procedures Bernie and Josh go through here have any relationship to reality—I utterly believe in their identities as TV technicians. A lot of this has to do with the specifics in the scene—things like Bernie chewing out Josh for not unplugging the power before he went in with cutters.

9. Here again you have a "because" (all right—a "'cause") that I think is unnecessary.

10. I don't think that you need, "What a loser." The expression on Bernie's face as Josh leaves will convey this without it being articulated. For the most part, comments characters make out loud to

themselves in naturalistic plays come across as arch and phony, particularly when the comments in question go on for longer than a word or two. People rarely talk out loud themselves. (Of course, there are some nonnaturalistic plays that establish the convention of characters talking to themselves. The key is that, indeed, the playwright clearly establishes at the top of the play the stylistic right for characters to express themselves in this way. For the most part in this book I'm dealing with naturalistic writing—attempting to create behavior for the stage or screen which will register on an audience as something that could happen in real life.)

11. I like this moment a lot because it relates back to an early passage— the bit about the self-locking door. Referring back to and building on elements introduced earlier in a scene gives a sense of tightness to writing, reinforcing the idea that the characters are operating in a concrete and consistent world.

12. Here, as elsewhere in the scene, there is strong use of negotiation over space. Part of what gives the scene its punch is that these guys are working in the house of a customer who isn't there. Obviously the customer, Mrs. Friedman, trusts them enough to leave her keys for them. The degree to which her trust isn't merited is part of what the scene is about. By placing into her TV a power source cannibalized from another TV, they are behaving in a way they would not if she were present.

13. At this point I think you're going into overkill, making explicit issue of ethics that you've raised organically and adroitly earlier in the scene. I don't think you need any of the discussion about what the Mormon customers would think of their behavior.

Though I've done some picking, technically this is a very impressive scene on several counts: it is mostly written in the present tense, it deals with negotiations over objects (the lock, the TV sets); the transformation of objects (the fact that the set gets fried in an accident and another set has to be cannibalized); negotiations over time, space, status, and values; and the tension between professional and private imperatives (Josh's need to get to the counselor versus his ethic as a TV repairman). As I mentioned, it also employs techniques (exposition through future tense, the disruption of convention and the violation of a setting) I will explore in lessons that follow.

And, to address the focus of this lesson: the high-context exposition here is very accomplished. We learn a great deal about these guys as a by-product of their going about their work: that they are repairmen making house calls, who some of their clients for the day have been, that Josh is married to Annie, that they have a child named Ted, and that there is sufficient trouble in the marriage to warrant a session with a social worker. We also get a very clear sense of the contrasting moralities of Josh and Bernie—that Bernie is more likely to do what is expedient and that Josh, though he goes along with Bernie, has some moral qualms. Where do I keep those gold stars?

By Larry Leinoff

(*Cluttered office. Sweetness and Gabe are seated at table. Multiple crushed cigarettes fill an ashtray between them.*)

SWEETNESS: What does the Tenth look like?

GABE: It's ours.

SWEETNESS: By how much?

GABE: Two points. Maybe three.[1]

SWEETNESS: That's too close. What about Mrs. Mendoza—were we out to her? Didn't we get an appropriation for Honduras? One of those countries. With all that rain. And the Church is also big down there. We're for school prayer. You might get Father— Father—what the hell is his name? Whatever it is—you might get him to say a word or two on the Senator's behalf.[2]

GABE: Kovic.

SWEETNESS: Yeah—Father Kovic. You talk to him. Kovic. That Polish? Didn't we get something for Poland? Ain't they in NATO now? We got them money for something. Check it out with Suzie.

GABE: No problem.

SWEETNESS: What about the Seventh?

GABE: Not so good. Riveredge really hurt us.[3]

SWEETNESS: Hey, our hands are clean.

GABE: The hell they are.

SWEETNESS: Gimme the paper.

(Gabe tosses Sweetness the paper. Sweetness scans page one, then opens it. He continues to read for a moment longer.)
Look at this—we're back on page three.

(Sweetness tosses the paper away in disgust.)
You know what people do with page three? They wrap fish in it.

GABE: We're four points down, Sweetness. I can show you the numbers.

SWEETNESS: Forget it. Who owes us in the Seventh? What about Wilcox?

GABE: I don't know.

SWEETNESS: Is he hiring?

GABE: I don't think so.

SWEETNESS: You get him on the phone. I wanna see twenty new slots or we'll send the inspectors in.

GABE: He's not gonna like that.[4]

SWEETNESS: You tell him.

(Pause.)
Hey—what about—what the hell is her name—Louise—Louise—

GABE: Spinelli?

SWEETNESS: Yeah. Ain't she in the Seventh?

GABE: Yeah.

SWEETNESS: Well, what about it? Did she ever get that kidney?

GABE: No.

SWEETNESS: Well—get her one. And I want it on video.

GABE: Where the hell am I gonna get a kidney?

SWEETNESS: How the hell do I know? You have two, don't you?

GABE: That's not funny.

SWEETNESS: There's a list for that stuff—right? She's on a list? Call up Doctor—who is that guy? See Suzie.[5] We built his fuckin' hospital—his fuckin' *research* hospital—and what has he found? Nothin'. What the hell are they doin' up there? Freakin' doctors. How many beds in the mausoleum? Four hundred, wasn't it? You can't tell me that with four hundred beds he can't find one extra kidney. I want Louise at the top of that list, and I want a camera crew out there when they wheel her in, and when they wheel her out.

GABE: You're pushin' it, Sweet.

SWEETNESS: You're damn right I am. We got four weeks. I wanna see Louise in three, walkin' into her kitchen carrying a big plate of lasagna. I want it on the evening news, and I want a puppy in the foreground wagging his tail.

1. Three swell clues. Reference to the "Tenth" could be a date or a district. The second line suggests a district to be more likely, and the mention of points in the third line nails it down. Very adroit.

2. Between "appropriation" and "We're for school prayer" and reference to the "Senator," we get that this concerns the reelection campaign of a United States Senator. There is a strong suggestion, too, that Sweetness and Gabe are city machine politicos. This sounds like urban turf they're working.

3. "Riveredge" sounds like a political scandal in which the Senator is currently embroiled.

4. This very neatly anticipates the next lesson in which I discuss doing exposition with the future tense.

5. The references to "Suzie" anticipate Lesson 14, on the use of indirect characterization. We're beginning to get a strong idea of Suzie's function in the organization and that she's probably as hard-nosed as these guys.

I think it would be hard to see this scene played without the word "cynical" occurring to a member of the audience. The credibility of the scene is enhanced by the specificity of the references; I not only believe these guys exist, I can see the world and people to which they refer.

10

LESSON

The Robin Hood Effect

STRANGE AS IT MAY SOUND, IT IS POSSIBLE TO DO EXPOSITION using the future tense.

Midway through David Mamet's *American Buffalo*, junk store proprietor Don and his low-life acquaintance Teach start collaborating on plans for a robbery. Don figures that if a recent customer in his shop gave him $90 for a nickel without turning a hair, then the guy probably has other valuable change stashed in his home. So Don discusses with Teach how to relieve the mark of his property.

Among the questions they discuss is who should be on the break-in team. Teach wants no part of Bobby, the slow-witted young drug addict who is a surrogate son to Don. Don relents on this point, but he feels there should be another man involved. He suggests Fletch. Teach objects to Fletch, too. He doesn't see the need for someone else on the job, and we strongly suspect that it's because Teach doesn't want to have to share the take with a third person.

The planning of the robbery is the central topic of the scene. Through the way they plan, Don and Teach's relationship and contrasting philosophies become distinct.

Mamet does something similar in the second scene of the first act of *Glengarry Glen Ross*. Moss and Aaronow simmer with resentment against the real estate concern for which they are salesmen. "Somebody should stand up and strike back," says Moss. What does Moss have in mind? Somebody should break into the office and steal the list of names of the most promising potential customers (also known as "the leads"). Moss' idea is to take this list and go to a competing real estate outfit and move to better jobs. As he talks, he offers justifications and rationalizations for the appropriateness of this action. Again, the by-product of the discussion is our deeper understanding of what drives Moss and Aaronow.

In the first scene of another Mamet play, *Speed-the-Plow*, two Hollywood executives (and self-professed "whores") named Fox and Gould plan the production of a prison movie that they know will be no good but will probably gross a fortune because a big star is willing to commit to playing the lead. Once more, what we glean from this scene are the values of the two men through the manner in which they discuss a joint undertaking.

What Mamet grasps is that you can tell a great deal about the content of people's characters through the future they hope to construct.

An analogy: You're watching a Robin Hood movie. Any Robin Hood movie. At some point there's always that shot of a flock of arrows in mid-flight as they descend upon the Sheriff of Nottingham and his thugs. From the trajectory of the arrows, you can not only make a pretty fair guess as to where the arrows will land, you also can make a pretty fair guess about from where they were fired. Just as you can mentally backtrack from those arrows in mid-flight to their source, you can often mentally backtrack from the plans people make to their source—the planners' values and personalities and their relationships to each other.

To refer back to the premises-and-conclusions model, if you give the audience the premise that your characters are planning this action, then the audience will draw conclusions about the kind of people who would make these plans in pursuit of this goal. The result: the audience will arrive at understandings about the backstory that you might otherwise have been tempted to write as more overt exposition.

One of the reasons we keep watching a film or a play is that we want to know what will happen next. Who is going to make what decision? Any passages that relate to how the characters intend to pursue their objectives are more likely to engage the audience's attention than recitations about what has gone before. Even mysteries, which involve the revelation of patterns from the past, are based on a question relating to the future: "Is Marlowe going to get to the bottom of this murder?" (This is one of the secrets of the power of the mystery form—it explores the past through forward action. Though Oedipus' problems started in the past, the action of the play is his moving forward with his investigation.)

As I've discussed, the writer is often tempted to resort to the past tense at the beginning of a script so as to let the audience know where these characters come from and what their circumstances are. After all, if you've invented rich pasts for them, you're going to want to share that invention. Typically, the first ten pages of a script by a developing writer have characters articulating much of their histories and circumstances.

In my experience, at about page ten, this writer probably is done with the introductions of characters needed to start the story. At about page ten, the action usually kicks in. And, at about page ten—surprise—the script springs to life. Having finished going over where they've been and what they've done (for the benefit of the eavesdropping audience), the characters start addressing what they hope to accomplish.

In fact, all that laying out of "necessary" information more often than not isn't necessary. This material is usually implicit in what the characters do now. The audience reasons that these characters wouldn't be engaged in this interaction if thus-and-such circumstances didn't pertain. You often don't need to set up the story. You can simply join the action of the story at a lively moment and trust that the audience will fill in most of the blanks. The audience is used to filling in the blanks. The audience has been trained in this skill since childhood. We often tune into a TV show or arrive at a movie several minutes late and still mostly we are able to pick up what's going on in a few minutes.

This isn't to say that writing those first ten pages is wasted effort. Those ten pages are like the scaffolding that a construction gang puts up when building a building—a system of platforms and supports designed to put the crew in position to be able to lay brick, paint, and so on. When the building is completed, the scaffolding is taken down.

The problem I often see in works by developing writers is that the scaffolding is left up. Those first ten pages that may have been very useful to begin the script may not be needed for the final script.

David Mamet is hardly the only dramatist to make dramatic use of plans. The TV series *Mission: Impossible* involved the concoction of another elaborate plan every week. Shaw's *Pygmalion* centers on Higgins and Pickering's plan to pass Eliza off as a lady at a royal ball. In *The Godfather*, key scenes involve the planning of crimes; notably Michael retrieving a gun planted behind a toilet in order to shoot his father's enemies.

Shakespeare, too, often shows his characters plotting. In a comic vein, much of the merriment in *Twelfth Night* and *Much Ado About Nothing* concerns plots to con Malvolio, Beatrice, and Benedick into taking the plunge into courtship.

But Shakespeare takes no backseat to Mamet when it comes to the plotting of crimes. *Macbeth* is one sustained conspiracy between the title character and his wife. Claudius plots with Laertes against his nephew in *Hamlet*. Iago plots against Cassio, Desdemona, and the title character in *Othello*. Shylock has his designs in *The Merchant of Venice*. Cassius and Brutus spend the first half of *Julius Caesar* working with half the cast to dispatch the title character.

One of my favorite passages in Shakespeare occurs in *King John* in a scene between the villainous John and his henchman, Hubert. John's young nephew Arthur is deemed by many to be the rightful king, and this irritates John, who takes Hubert aside in act III, scene iii and opens his mind to him:

KING JOHN: Good Hubert, Hubert, Hubert, throw thine eye
On yon young boy. I'll tell thee what, my friend,
He is a very serpent in my way;
And wheresoe'er this foot of mine doth tread,
He lies before me. Dost thou understand me?
Thou art his keeper.

HUBERT: And I'll keep him so
That he shall not offend your Majesty.

KING JOHN: Death.

HUBERT: My lord?

KING JOHN: A grave.

HUBERT: He shall not live.

KING JOHN: Enough!
I could be merry now. Hubert, I love thee.

Is there anywhere in dramatic literature a murder more economically proposed and confirmed? "I could be merry now." By his brutal, cheerful brevity, we know John for what he is.

Setting up plans may also be dramatically useful because doing so sets up expectations that the writer may harvest by making their execution go awry. Crime films frequently center around criminals whose brilliant heists and capers are undone—*Heat, Double Indemnity, Asphalt Jungle,* and so on. In both *American Buffalo* and *Glengarry,* the burglaries are failures, and King John's plotting has consequences that feature Shakespeare in his most ironic mode. (No, I'm not going to tell you what happens. It's a great satiric play and worth reading.)

Most poignant of all are the plans unrealized. "Tell me about the rabbits," Lennie keeps asking George in John Steinbeck's *Of Mice and Men.* Lennie and George—and Blanche and Willie Loman and the other characters on stage and screen who have unrealized scenarios for attaining better lives—are all the more moving because they have mapped out modest schemes to find safe havens. The saying from which Steinbeck took his title begins, "The best-laid plans of mice and men . . ."

Here's how I employed this technique in an early scene between the two men in *Flyovers.*

OLIVER: Would fifty bucks be useful?

TED: For what?

OLIVER: You were talking before about a plaque. For Mr. Kelly when he retires.

TED: That's generous.

OLIVER: Well, what the hell, he was always nice to me. So, what do you figure for the inscription?

TED: Inscription?

OLIVER: On the plaque. Something about the occasion or the purpose or whatever.

TED: You're the writer—what do you think?

OLIVER: OK—"To Mr. Kelly in acknowledgment of, uh, recognition of uh, with thanks for—" how many years?

TED: Thirty-six.

OLIVER: "—thirty-six years of inspiration as a teacher and a friend." Something like that. Maybe an engraving of a test tube or a Bunsen burner.

TED: Sure, that ought to bring a tear to his eye.

Here was my thinking as I wrote this passage: Talk by grown men of a plaque for someone to whom they refer to as "Mr. Kelly" suggests that Kelly is someone they have in common (you're not likely to confer on a plaque for someone you don't know) and that he was an authority figure from the past. In soliciting Oliver's input on the wording of the inscription, Ted has a well-supported reason for referring to Oliver being a writer. It becomes clear that Kelly is one of their former teachers as Oliver improvises what the inscription might be, and the reference to the Bunsen burner suggests that Kelly taught science. The passage invites a further inference—in fact, the most important one—that Ted and Oliver were classmates in high school.

Notice I haven't had either actually say they were classmates in high school. Rather, this is the inference to which their planning the plaque logically leads. So, they talk about the future (designing and getting a plaque for Kelly), but the audience gleans from this something about their shared past.

> **Assignment Ten:** Invent a scene between two people in which we discover much of their past or given circumstances through the plans they make.

By Deborah Medwin

> (*Karen and Tara sit on a couch. On the coffee table in front of Karen is a bag of weed. Karen cleans, keeping her head down. Every now and then she looks at Tara with irritation. Tara, oblivious, holds the bat[1] like a cigarette, gesturing with it as she talks, but not smoking.*)

TARA: It's twenty minutes to Dockers.

KAREN: Since when?

TARA: If I drive.[2]

KAREN: You're not driving. I'm driving and I'm not going to Dockers. It's too far.

TARA: There won't be a soul at the Publick House.[3]

KAREN: I can tell you what will happen if we go to Dockers. I'll pay twenty bucks to stand in a crowded room with strangers I don't like, listening to music I can't stand and drinking beer I can't afford.

TARA: The point is to meet a man who *can* afford it! Then they take you to quiet places with good food and expensive wine.[4]

KAREN: Are you going to smoke that?

TARA: Here.

(Tara passes her the half-smoked bat.)

KAREN: Finish it.

(Tara begins to light it but starts on a new idea instead.)

TARA: Publick House is good during the week. On the weekends, if you want to meet someone you have to go to the clubs. You have to dress up, put on makeup and spend a little money. Otherwise your only choices are the guys who are too cheap to pay a twenty-dollar cover, and personally I have no time for them.[5]

KAREN: Smoke that!

TARA: What is this—a race? Let me enjoy it.

KAREN: It's not a cigarette.

TARA: What's not?

KAREN: Don't smoke it like it was a cigarette. Finish the hit and pass it back.

TARA: Jesus Christ! Can I enjoy it please?

(Tara takes a hit, passes it over.)

KAREN: Thank you.

TARA: I don't have the same lung capacity. Jesus.

KAREN: Sorry. I'd just like to get high, too.[6]

TARA: So, can we go to Dockers?

KAREN: I'm not driving home drunk.

TARA: I'll drive.

KAREN: Oh. That'll make a difference.[7]

TARA: Are you going to fill me a hit?

KAREN: Are you going to come to the Publick House with me?

TARA: It's so boring there.

KAREN: If I fill this, will you smoke it in one hit?

TARA: Are we going to Dockers?

KAREN: No.

TARA: Then no.[8]

    (Tara grabs the bat from Karen.)

I'd rather stay home and get high.

KAREN: Oh, that's fun.

TARA: What's the difference? We'll only talk to each other anyway. It's cheaper.[9]

KAREN: We won't have to get dressed.[10]

TARA: We could rent a movie.

KAREN: I could roll us individual joints.

TARA: This is why we never meet anyone.

KAREN: There's never anyone worth meeting anyway.[11]

1. For the benefit of readers, I am informed that this is a piece of drug-smoking paraphernalia.

2. "If I drive" suggests that Tara believes she is the faster and better driver. This exchange also hints at Tara's objective—to get Karen to agree to join her in going to Dockers.

3. Their night life seems to consist of two alternatives—Dockers and the Publick House, and Tara's comments suggest that Dockers is the more happening place.

4. More pieces fall into place: they're both single and looking, and neither has money. Dockers is a place where women who are single and without money can go and hope to hook up with better-heeled guys who will be generous. The hitch is they have to have enough money for the $20 cover at Dockers. By implication, there is no cover at the Publick House. By implication, too, the men at the Publick House, not being able to afford the cover at Dockers (otherwise they'd be there, right?), are not prime catches from an economic point of view.

5. In supporting her case for Dockers versus the Publick House, Tara has license to explain more of the setup of the single scene in this area. Also, from the driving times mentioned and the limited opportunities outlined, I get the impression that this is set outside of the city. (I was subsequently informed by the author that the places in question are in the Hamptons on Long Island.)

6. Good negotiation over an object. Karen is deflecting discussion about where to go tonight by starting a quarrel. Her impatience with the subject of going out has been transformed into impatience with the way Tara deals with the dope.

7. A good indication of Karen's view of Tara's drinking habits and driving ability.

8. Good overt negotiation—Karen will oblige Tara's dope pleasures if Tara will oblige Karen's preference for the Publick House.

9. Here we get the idea that no matter what the setting, the two of them don't have much optimism about finding worthwhile company.

10. A compromise is going to be reached. This is underscored by their quick agreement on an alternate plan to going to either Dockers or the Publick House.

11. Nice final line. Raises the question of whether an outside eye would view *them* as being worth meeting.

The scene is generally a very efficiently rendered picture of two young women on a weekend night, unattached and not harboring much hope. The limited nature of the plans they discuss suggests the limited world they inhabit. Tara also registers as being slightly more hopeful than Karen. Tara is willing to take an action. Karen seems to be rather depressed.

This also sounds like a negotiation that has gone on before. Having effectively established this as a typical night for the two of them, now it would be up to the writer to come up with dramatic action that would make this evening unique. We don't watch a play or a movie to see a night much like any other, but to see what is different about *this* night that the writer chooses to make us privy to it. So something will disrupt what would be the ordinary progress of this evening.

For another example of this technique in practice take a look at the scenes between Sara and Bill and Judy and Bill in response to Assignment 7. The techniques I'm introducing are not something that are to be employed one at a time; they often are used in combination. The Sara-Bill-Judy scenes work both as scenes that bring out Bill's different and mutually exclusive voices and as scenes based on the Robin Hood principle.

By Nicholas Wardigo

(*An autobody shop. Tools and car parts are strewn everywhere. There is a desk with an appointment book sitting on it. There is also a chair purposefully set up with a small table next to it. Carl, in his twenties, is behind the desk with a scrub brush, scrubbing his face and hands. Mrs. Santos, in her late forties, enters with a large handbag.*)

CARL: Mrs. Santos! Man, am I glad to see you!

MRS. SANTOS: Always a pleasure, Carl. But first things first.

CARL: What? Oh, right.

(*Carl pages through the appointment book.*)

CARL: How does Tuesday sound?[1]

MRS. SANTOS: Tuesday? I didn't rush down here to be insulted.

CARL: Oh, right. Sorry. Monday, then? How about Monday?

MRS. SANTOS: Sunday.

CARL: Sunday?

MRS. SANTOS: That's what I said.

CARL: But we're booked solid.[2]

MRS. SANTOS: Well, then, it looks like you wasted both our time.
(*Mrs. Santos starts to exit.*)

CARL: Wait! All right. Sunday. I'll squeeze you in somehow. Just an oil change, right?

MRS. SANTOS: Inspection.

CARL: What!? That could take hours!

MRS. SANTOS: Sure could.

CARL: Cut me a break, here.

MRS. SANTOS: You called me. What do you want to do?[3]

(Carl studies the appointment book.)

CARL: I can't, Mrs. Santos. I just can't.

MRS. SANTOS: What time did you say your lady-friend was coming over?[4]

(Carl looks at his watch, looks at Mrs. Santos, and looks at the appointment book.)

CARL: Sunday?

MRS. SANTOS: Sunday.

CARL: Morning?

MRS. SANTOS: I have tea with the ladies after church.[5]

CARL: One o'clock?

MRS. SANTOS: Perfect.

CARL: Done.

MRS. SANTOS: Where should I set up?

CARL: Over there.

(Carl points to the chair and table. Mrs. Santos plops her handbag on the table and pulls out scissors, combs, hair gel, manicure supplies, etc. Carl scribbles out several names in the appointment book and pencils something into the margins. He rushes over to the chair and sits. Mrs. Santos ties a huge plastic hairdresser's bib around his neck.)

MRS. SANTOS: Where you taking her?

CARL: Fellicia's.

MRS. SANTOS: That place on Robinson?

CARL: Yeah. Right across from the bank.

MRS. SANTOS: Must be a pretty girl.[6]

CARL: You can't even imagine.

MRS. SANTOS: Honey, what have you done to your face?[7]

CARL: Nothing. Why?

MRS. SANTOS: Looks like you took a Brillo pad to it.

CARL: It was covered in grease. She just called an hour ago, and I had to get it off. Why? Does it look bad?

MRS. SANTOS: I got a mud pack that'll take care of it.

CARL: How much?

MRS. SANTOS: Tire rotation.[8]

CARL: Tire rotation?

MRS. SANTOS: One . . . tire . . . rotation.

CARL: Can't do it. Not on Sunday.

MRS. SANTOS: How pretty is this girl?

CARL (*Thinking*): Sounds awful steep.

MRS. SANTOS: I'll throw in a manicure.

CARL: We got time?

(*Mrs. Santos lifts up Carl's arm and looks at his watch.*)

MRS. SANTOS: Just enough.

CARL: Done.

(*Mrs. Santos pulls a jar of mud out of her bag and spreads it over Carl's face.*)

MRS. SANTOS: Fellicia's, huh? Got reservations?

CARL: Yeah.

MRS. SANTOS: When did you call them?

CARL: Right after I called you.

MRS. SANTOS: Surprised you got in on such short notice.

CARL: Yeah. Pretty lucky.

MRS. SANTOS: Even so. Last minute on a Friday night. That place is usually booked weeks ahead of time.

CARL: I know the owner.

MRS. SANTOS: What did it cost you?

CARL: Bleed his radiator.[9]

MRS. SANTOS: Pick of the menu?

CARL: Plus dessert and coffee after.

MRS. SANTOS: Not bad. Must be an awful pretty girl.[10]

CARL: You can't even imagine.

1. My hunch is the scene could start with this line. We have an under-
   standable tendency to start scenes when characters make entrances,

but most scenes that begin this way start with the exchange of pleasantries that don't contribute much. Better, in my opinion, to start when people have something at stake. And indeed, the scene really gets under way with, "How does Tuesday sound?"

2. By now, the audience has probably figured out that they're negotiating over scheduling, and because of the setting, that it probably has to do with servicing her car.

3. The fact that he called her suggests that this will involve an exchange of favors.

4. Now we get the idea that the favor he wants from her has to do with him preparing for a date. It is apparently sufficient to motivate him to compromise.

5. This detail gives us a suggestion of the sort of life she leads—one in which church and related rituals play an important part.

6. Her response suggests that Fellicia's is a place likely to impress, probably expensive.

7. Though she has done some hard bargaining with him, her concern reveals a maternal side. His response suggests that he is falling into the voice he uses with his own mother.

8. How quickly they shift from a mother-son pattern to hard-nosed bargaining!

9. I love the economy of exchanges here: "Bleed his radiator." "Pick of the menu?" "Plus dessert and coffee after."

10. You probably don't need the "Not bad." That will be conveyed by the expression on the performer's face and will be implicit in the line she does say.

The scene is not only charming in itself (especially in the shifts between the hard-nosed negotiating and the more personal voices), it also nicely suggests something of the nature of this community, particularly the part bartering plays in it. Without actually seeing more of the neighborhood, one gets a sense of its cohesion and human dimension. Nice, subtle work.

SIDEBAR 4

Logic

IT SEEMS THAT SOME PEOPLE WENT TO SEE A SECOND CITY SHOW, not knowing the kind of evening they were in for. After the performance, they ran into a cast member in the lobby. They told him they liked the show fine. One of them added, "At first, I found the plot a little confusing, but by the end of the evening I figured it out."

Now, the form of the typical show at Second City is a revue. Actors play a variety of characters in a collection of scenes over the course of an evening. There is no plot.

But this member of the audience, assuming for some reason that he was there to watch a play, insisted on seeing a narrative where none existed.

The desire to make sense of things is central to the human condition. Religion and science both arose to help create some kind of order out of the constant onslaught of the bewildering. Indeed, in some societies, religion and science were the same. (In primitive cultures, night and day were not comprehended as the consequence of the earth spinning on its axis, but rather the product of an eternal and ongoing contest between gods.) One of Aristotle's many accomplishments was the popularization of the idea that, with proper analysis, you could figure out in which category anything belonged and its relationship to everything else.

When they go to the theatre or the movies, people bring with them this compulsion to make sense out of what they see. They look to discern some sort of order or scheme in the series of actions the actors place before them. To satisfy this drive, as my Second City story attests, some will even go so far as to impose an order of their own devising.

I suggest that, since the audience is going to look for a logic, it usually is a good idea to supply something for them to find.

A script generally prescribes a series of events to be enacted. These events are presented in a specified order. The fact that one thing happens, then a second thing happens, and then a third thing happens suggests that the second thing happens *because* the first thing happened, and the third happens *because* the first and second took place. In other words, the audience looks for causality. A dramatic action is necessarily rooted in a prior action. A script doesn't propose a bunch of events in a random sequence; the events are given much of their meaning by the sequence in which they take place or are presented.

We writers are responsible for providing the logic that makes the events and the order in which they unfold appear credible and inevitable.

This is a tall order and one that some of my younger students have difficulty filling. Perhaps it's due to growing up with rock videos. The typical video does not deal with a progression of events but with a bombardment of visuals suggested by a song. The effect can be exciting and startling, but its example has little to teach about the building of longer narrative structures. I think I see its influence in some of my students' tendencies to go for the quick image, often a jarring and unsupported burst of violence. (If people in society used deadly force as often as my students do in their scenes, we would swim in a sea of blood.)

Many high-profile movies also seem to be composed as a series of set pieces tenuously threaded together. An action director decides it would be fun to shoot a sequence in which two characters duel from the roofs of two elevators zooming side by side up the outside of a building, and the writer is asked to find a way to fit this into the structure of the picture. In other words, instead of the sequence arising organically out of the script, the script is shaped around what somebody thinks would be cool. The result is movies like *Mission: Impossible* and the *Batman* series—anthologies of cool ideas that contain little by way of coherent plots. (These movies are not unlike the early musical comedies. Lorenz Hart and Richard Rodgers once jammed a number saluting the Roxy Music Hall into a show set in Hungary because they thought the evening could use a zippy song at that point. It didn't seem to bother them or anybody else that the Roxy Music Hall had nothing to do with Hungary.

This way of working changed when Oscar Hammerstein II replaced Hart as Rodgers' collaborator.)

But let's say that you do indeed come up with a series of events that seem to build in a persuasive way, there is still another kind of logic that must be addressed: the internal logic of every single character in the piece.

One of my students was working on a Western about a corrupt lawman who tries to get a gunslinger to provoke the head of a bandit gang into a deadly confrontation. I asked him why the gunslinger would agree to confront the gang leader.

"So that they have a fight and the gunslinger gets killed."

"That's *your* reason for the fight," I said. "What's the gunslinger's reason for picking the quarrel?"

"Because the lawman wants him to."

"Why does he agree to do what the lawman wants him to?"

"Because the lawman wants these two guys to fight 'cuz he figures one of them will get killed."

"But why," I asked, "does the gunslinger agree to do this? Does he know how dangerous the gang leader is?"

"Yes."

"Does he have a personal reason to confront the gang leader?"

"No."

"So he's confronting someone who could kill him—who *will* kill him in your story—because somebody else wants him to, not because he has any stake in confronting him."

"But, you see, there's this *fight*."

"Does he owe the lawman anything?"

"No. The lawman's new in town."

"Why does the lawman have any reason to believe that this guy, whom he apparently barely knows, at his prompting would do something that is obviously suicidal?"

The student was mystified by these questions. He couldn't understand my objections. All he knew was my pickiness was interfering with his plan to build to this swell gun battle. The fact that he hadn't provided any motivation for the combatants to take each other on didn't register as being remotely relevant.

All right, this is an extreme case.

But time and again I see a similar battle between these two impulses—the writer's impulse to make the story he wants to tell happen as opposed to the impulses of the characters taking actions consistent with their characters, resources, and objectives. Very often, I get the sense that the characters are being pushed around by the writers. The result is that the focus is on the writer's intentions at the expense of the believ-ability of the characters.

I think if I'm doing my job properly, during the performance a member of the audience gets lost in the illusion that the characters I've created are living, breathing, and unique souls behaving in ways credibly related to their wants and needs. Only after the story has been told do I want the audience to slip into a critical mode and appreciate logic of the piece's structure.

I don't think it is overstating to say that dramatic writing is a disci-pline calling for self-induced schizophrenia. I think you must be able to simultaneously inhabit the perspectives not only of all of your charac-ters, but, without forgetting your own perspective as the architect of the structure, also anticipate what the thought processes of the audience are likely to be. In the end, one should be able to read the script following the through-lines of each of the characters as well as be able to step back and find satisfaction in the work's overall shape.

One must make the logic of the tale and the logic the characters com-plement each other.

11
LESSON

Disruption of a Ritual

IN WRITER-DIRECTOR GEORGE SEATON'S FILM THE COUNTERFEIT
Traitor, Lilli Palmer plays Marianne Mollendorf, a German woman passing
along military information to the Allies during World War II. Her motives
for spying are religious; she is a Catholic and she thinks Hitler is the
Antichrist. Midway through the film, on the basis of some of her information, the Allies launch a bombing raid which goes awry and results in the
deaths of a number of children. Guilt-ridden, Marianne goes to church to
confess her responsibility.

But the Gestapo have been watching her and, seeing her approach the
church, they distract the priest while one of their agents takes his place
in the confessional. Sitting in the penitent's compartment, she pours out
her heart through the latticework to what she thinks is a man of God.
Wanting more details, the masquerading agent asks a question about the
names of her associates. The camera records her realization that the
question could not have been asked by a priest. She knows she has just
doomed herself.

The power of the scene is rooted in the Gestapo's abuse of the sanctity
of the confessional. They have violated a holy rite, transforming its purpose from one of moral and spiritual cleansing to the purposes of state-
sanctioned murder.

Formal rituals and ceremonies prescribe behavior, usually for a solemn
or holy purpose. Their very rigidity makes disrupting them a tempting dramatic strategy.

Weddings in plays and films almost never go as the characters plan.

Shakespeare disrupts a marriage ceremony twice in *Much Ado About Nothing*. In act IV, scene i, the company gathers for what is supposed to be the marriage of Claudio and a young woman named Hero, daughter of Leonato. But the villainous Don John has led Claudio to believe that Hero has been trysting with someone else. No sooner does Leonato give his daughter away to Claudio according to the protocols of the ceremony than Claudio shocks the assemblage by giving her back, refusing to marry her and using her supposed wantonness as justification. What began as a wedding turns into a scene of cruelty and accusation, stirring up the potential for tragedy. (Indeed, Shakespeare would transform elements of this plot into tragedy by remaking Don John as Iago, Hero as Desdemona, and Claudio as the title character of *Othello*.)

In act V, scene iv, Claudio makes good on his promise to marry a masked lady of Leonato's choosing to make restitution for his part in causing the grief he believes led to Hero's death. Once the ceremony is completed, the mysterious bride drops her mask and is revealed to be Hero, alive and well. Again, a wedding has been disrupted, this time for comic effect.

So, the disruption of a ritual has the potential of releasing either drama or comedy.

Let's look a bit more closely at the comic potential of disrupting a wedding ceremony. Quite a few pieces use the disruption of weddings as a device for rescuing someone from what the audience knows to be an inappropriate match. Philip Barry's *The Philadelphia Story* is concerned with a woman named Tracy who comes to realize, just as she's about to wed a stuffed shirt, that she's really still in love with her ex-husband, Dexter (who happens to be in the neighborhood). The film *It Happened One Night* (directed by Frank Capra from a Robert Riskin screenplay based on a novelette by Samuel Hopkins Adams called *Night Bus*) builds to the point when Ellie (played by Claudette Colbert) walks down the aisle on her father's arm as he coaxes her to ditch the guy she's about to get hitched to and run off with the guy he knows she's really nuts about, Peter (played by Clark Gable). In both of these cases, the ceremony is disrupted before it can be completed.

In contrast, to return again to the end of *The Graduate*, Benjamin (Dustin Hoffman) arrives at the church only to find that the ceremony has been completed and Elaine (Katherine Ross) is already legally married. Seeing

Benjamin, Elaine flees the altar, leaving her husband behind. Elaine's mother, Mrs. Robinson (Anne Bancroft) grabs her wrist, saying, "Elaine—it's too late." "Not for me," says Elaine, pulling away. And of course, part of the point of this moment is that according to the ethics of a previous time (and in a movie of a previous time), it would have indeed been too late. The fact that Elaine can liberate herself a second after her marriage to another has been formally accomplished vividly conveys her release from the ethics of her parents' world.

Many of Shakespeare's comedies end either with marriage or the promise of marriage between the romantic leads, a convention that has been embraced in countless scripts since. A wedding at the end of a show gives formal emphasis to the impression that a piece's conclusion is in a world that has achieved harmony and unity.

Leave it to Caryl Churchill, in *Mad Forest*, to stand this convention on its head. The play leads to the wedding of a Romanian bride and groom who come from different ethnic groups. In the play's last scene, during the wedding reception, their families get drunk, cultural frictions flare, and what was planned as a celebration of love turns into a brawl. Written in 1990, only a few months after the fall of Ceausescu's repressive reign, Churchill was prescient in her prediction that many of the people of the countries of eastern Europe, rather than uniting in common purpose in the wake of the fall of Communism, would rekindle ethnic animosities and turn on each other. To dramatize this through the disruption of a wedding is a characteristically brilliant stroke from this bold writer.

Funerals, too, are ripe for disruption, and, of course, Shakespeare makes good use of them. Marc Antony's funeral oration in *Julius Caesar* turns an occasion of mourning into the inciting of a murderous mob, and Ophelia's funeral in *Hamlet* explodes in a confrontation between the prince and Ophelia's brother, Laertes.

Sophocles made notable use of a disrupted funeral in *Antigone*. Creon, the king, decrees that the body of the rebel Polynices must not be allowed the dignity of a burial and that anybody who disobeys his order is to be executed. The person who challenges him is his niece, the title character, an action that precipitates the play's tragic action.

Usually being the most solemn of occasions, there is enormous comic potential in the disruption of a funeral.

A famous Second City scene directed by Del Close features a group of mourners trying to maintain decorum despite the fact that the deceased met his end in a bizarre accident involving an economy-sized can of Van Camp's beans. In the scene's last moments, while the guests stuff handkerchiefs into their mouths in order to keep from exploding into laughter, his widow talks of finding her husband rushing blindly around the kitchen with the bean can jammed on his head, and her futile attempt to get him to an opener in time.

At the end of *The Wrong Box* (directed by Bryan Forbes from a screenplay by Larry Gelbart and Burt Shevelove and based on a novel by Robert Louis Stevenson and Lloyd Osbourne), the confusion in a cemetery triggers a slapstick sequence that makes another grieving widow howl with laughter.

Francis Ford Coppola and Mario Puzo's movies based on *The Godfather* derive much of their power from the juxtaposition of sacred ceremonies and murderous doings. The first sequence in *The Godfather* shows Vito Corleone (Marlon Brando) planning crimes in a dark room of his mansion as the guests dance at his daughter's wedding outside. In *The Godfather, Part II*, Michael Corleone (Al Pacino) wordlessly authorizes the murder of his own brother Fredo (John Cazale) during the funeral of their mother.

I've focused on the use that has been made of disrupting weddings and funerals, but there is similar opportunity in the disruption of any formal rite or service—a trial, a baptism, the investing of a knighthood, an execution, a Japanese tea ceremony, and so on. As I mentioned in *The Dramatist's Toolkit*, to violate the integrity of what the audience recognizes as the normal course of a structured proceeding releases theatrical energy in much the same way that splitting an atom releases nuclear energy.

Assignment Eleven: Write a scene in which an established ceremony or ritual is disrupted.

By Kathy Monk

EXT. BACKYARD—DAY

A birthday cake with many unlit candles. STAN, an elderly man, sits behind it. Next to him, RUTH, an elderly woman. Unopened gifts sit on the table. The day is grey.

TWO CHILDREN are playing in the yard.

TERRY and CRAIG, a middle-aged couple, exchange a look, then sit opposite Stan and Ruth at the table.

CRAIG

Maybe we should sing now, Pop. It looks like the sky's getting darker.

A beat.

RUTH

Let's wait awhile. Tony said he'd be here. That storm's still over the lake.

Craig calls to the kids.

CRAIG

Hey guys, do you want to sing to Grandpa now?

STAN

We're gonna wait a little longer.[1] I can wait. You don't have someplace to go, do ya? It's Sunday, you didn't say you had to be somewhere.

CRAIG

No, Pop, I don't have to be anywhere. It's just that we've been waiting awhile and with this storm . . . we're not even sure Tony's coming. He might have gotten held up—doin' something with Willie. He could've have lost track of time. You know how those two are when they get together. Maybe he forgot.

The kids run to the table.

KIDS

Ice cream and cake! Ice cream and cake!

TERRY

No, not yet. When Uncle Tony decides to show up.

The kids whine and run off.

STAN

Tony called yesterday and said he'd be here. I called him in the morning and he said he'd be pretty busy all weekend, but he'd make it today. He wants to see the kids. You know he's got a new job. I think he's supposed to start tomorrow. We'll find out when he gets here.[2]

CRAIG

I haven't really talked to Tony in awhile. I didn't know anything about the job.

RUTH

What is it with you two? I can't believe you didn't ask him about his new job. What do you boys talk about?[3]

CRAIG

We don't see each other that much, Ma. I try to call him, but—

TERRY

Craig can't always track Tony down. And, you know, after Tony walked out on that job Craig got him with the builders, we really don't want to hear about his jobs anymore.[4]

Looking at the kids.

The kids would really like to sing now. They've been waiting long enough for ice cream and cake, don't you think?

> STAN

The kids are playing, let 'em have fun—they don't care. It's my birthday and I want both my sons here. It might be my last one and—

> RUTH

Stan! Don't say that!

> STAN

I'll say and do what I damn well please!

Looking directly at Terry.

I said we're gonna wait for Tony. What's a birthday without the kids?

> CRAIG

The kids are—

> STAN

My kids!

Terry stands.

> TERRY

One of your kids is here, but that doesn't seem to matter to you. You can wait for Tony all night if you like. I'm taking my kids home.

Turns.

Let's go, guys.

> KIDS

Aw, Mom—we want ice cream and cake!

There's a flash of lightning. The sound of thunder.

> CRAIG

I think we waited too long.

1. Notice that up to this point in the scene, almost all of the lines have been future tense. Good use of the Robin Hood effect.

2. This feels a little exposition-heavy, beginning with, "You know he's got a new job." Starting a sentence with "you know" frequently signals that what follows is going to be the delivery of information for the sake of the author.

3. I've got a bit of a prejudice against lines that begin "I can't believe." It's another pretty certain signal that exposition is on its way. More often than not, you can cut the "I can't believe" and turn the rest of the line into a question. "You didn't ask him about his new job?" properly delivered will imply "I can't believe."

4. And there's another "you know" signalling the introduction of forced exposition.

Mostly, I think you've accomplished the assignment well. The disruption of the birthday party reveals the fissures in the family efficiently.

My suggestion would have been to have them try to *do* something about Tony's absence—maybe figure out where they might phone to get a line on where he is. Where they phone would give us a sense of the dimensions of Tony's life, the other pulls on his loyalty and time.

Whenever possible, try to put the characters into situations in which they take actions rather than discuss their situation. You can make their situation more vivid by the actions they contemplate taking.

By Donald Andreasen

(*A room at a funeral parlor.*[1] *Guy, 36, and Gail, 32, are sitting in seats.*)[2]

GUY (*Spotting someone offstage*): Oh my god, it's her.

GAIL: Well, go over and talk to her.

GUY: I can't do that here.

GAIL: Why not?

GUY: It's Grandma's funeral for God's sake.[3] I'm supposed to be mourning.

GAIL: You are mourning.

GUY: How's it going to look if I saunter over . . .[4]

GAIL: Go talk to her already.

GUY: What am I going to say?

GAIL: Tell her "thank you for coming."

GUY: Oooo, that's a good one. What else?

GAIL: I don't know. What do you normally say to women?

GUY: I don't really talk to women. I mean, I do when I have to— like at work, that's easy. Socially? I stammer, honk, wheeze—

GAIL: What are you worried about? She's a nice girl and you're a nice guy. Don't worry. Maybe it's destiny.

GUY: Her coming to the funeral?

GAIL: You never know.

GUY: What if I go over and say that?

GAIL: Say what?

GUY: You know, "our meeting here today seems like destiny."

GAIL: You can't tell *her* that.[5] It's got to be subtle.

GUY: I can't do it.

GAIL: If you like her . . .

GUY: I do.

GAIL: Then . . .

GUY: I can't.

(*Makes wheezing and honking sounds.*)

GAIL: Whatever.

GUY: Maybe later.

GAIL: A little later and you'll end up like Grandma.

GUY: I'm only 36 for Christ's sake. Did Mother put you up to this?

GAIL: Of course not. I just want to see you . . .[6]

GUY: I am happy.

GAIL: No you're not.

GUY (*Burying his head in his hands*): I know.

GAIL: You need a woman.

GUY: You're telling me????

GAIL: So talk to . . . hey, look she's going up front. Now's your chance.

GUY: What?

GAIL: Go ahead.

GUY: She's kneeling in front of the casket!

GAIL: Well, she's alone.

GUY: I can't talk to her there.

GAIL: Don't worry, Grandma can't hear you.

GUY: She's gonna think I'm a . . .

GAIL: You gotta be more aggressive.

GUY: I'll pick my spot.

GAIL: You'll wait too long.

GUY: Will you lay off?

GAIL: Hey, you're the one whining about not having a girlfriend all the time. I'm just trying to help.

GUY: Just don't push me, that's all.

GAIL: Fine.

GUY: I'll talk to her.

GAIL: All right.

GUY: I got to wait for the right moment.

1. Don't forget that sound can also help establish a scene. If they're at a funeral parlor, odds are some kind of appropriate music is playing. Some writers go so far as to suggest specific pieces of music. Do be aware, though, that if you suggest a recording of a pop song (e.g., "Bridge over Troubled Water" by Paul Simon), a deal has to be made and royalties have to be paid for the use of that song in performance. In a case such as this scene, one could probably get a musician friend to record a piece of appropriate music in the public domain.

2. Specifying how they are dressed could also be useful. These days, when casual dress is the norm, even in most professional work places, to see people dressed in black suits is even more of a tip-off that we're witnessing one of those occasions that compel more

formal wear. Between the music and what they wear, you might be able to communicate what's going on without a word being said.

3. It probably doesn't strain credibility for him to explicitly label the ceremony they're attending. I have a hunch, though, there might be a way of getting across that it's Grandmother's funeral without using the word "funeral." The music (if you use it), their clothing, and the setting have done half of the work. There's a good chance you'll get a laugh if the audience figures out for themselves that Grandmother is lying in a coffin not far away.

4. This is a matter of personal preference, but I think lines that are supposed to be interrupted should end with a dash |—| and lines that are supposed to trail off without interruption should end with | . . . |. Such choices in punctuation signal to the actors something of the pacing you intend for the scene and, so, something of the scene's subtext.

5. This passage uses the negotiation over the future nicely.

6. When one character is in the process of saying something that another character (or the audience) can finish, I think it is indeed a good tactic to have the line be interrupted and finished by someone else, as you have done here. I'm sure that everybody in the audience knows where "I just want to see you . . ." is heading, so having Guy anticipate the word with his line, "I am happy," suggests that Guy is as impatient as the audience likely is with the cliché, which has the effect of neutralizing the audience's impatience.

Using a funeral—and the funeral of a loved relative, yet—as the occasion for a pickup is an engaging conceit. As I suggest above, because they are designated as solemn and sad occasions, funerals prescribe particularly restricted and dignified behavior. One of the ways in which writer David Mamet and director Sidney Lumet (adapting the novel by Barry Reed) establish the character of the lawyer Paul Newman plays in The Verdict is by having Newman show up at the funerals of strangers and attempt to solicit business from mourners. That he would go so far is an index of how lost he is at the beginning of the film, setting a low point against which his subsequent moral reclamation is all the more impressive.

A ritual is a manifestation of the values of the society or institution from which it sprang. To disrupt a ritual can be a dramatic way to show how alienated the violator is from that society or institution.

12
LESSON

Disruption of Routine or Convention

IN THE LAST LESSON, I DISCUSSED THE DRAMATIC OPPORTUNITIES offered by disrupting an established ceremony or ritual.

But not only formal events are ripe for disruption. Any established pattern of behavior may be disrupted to useful dramatic effect. This can take the form of subverting a professional procedure, undermining the audience's expectations of a genre, or altering a few words of what would otherwise be a clichéd phrase or the expression of a tired idea. Any of these tactics may jar an audience out of complacency.

The TV series *Lou Grant* concerns itself with the workings of a Los Angeles newspaper. A particularly effective episode called "Blackout," written by Steve Kline, shows the staff of the paper trying to put out an edition when the power goes out. The bulk of the show describes how they improvise to accomplish what needs to be done—lighting candles, rummaging for manual typewriters to complete their stories, finding a printer located in an area of Los Angeles unaffected by the blackout that is capable of physically producing the paper on schedule, and so on. By showing how the series' regular characters cope with the problems, many of the aspects of putting out a paper that in other episodes are invisible—taken for granted because they are routine—suddenly are front and center. By the end of the episode, the audience understands better the mechanics of what it takes to produce a daily paper. In fact, the audience appreciates it better than if the episode had shown a day in which everything ran smoothly.

Whenever the status quo is disturbed, the very act of people having to cope with the disturbance necessarily conveys details of the status that was quo. This can be useful if you want to do exposition about the normal routine of characters in a given environment without putting the audience to sleep by showing it.

Los Angeles has an earthquake. (Don't jump to any conclusions about my using Los Angeles in two examples in a row.) Chunks of the freeway slam to the earth. Flimsy apartment buildings buckle. Utilities are disrupted. Schools are closed. Middle-class people accustomed to the comfort of their homes have to camp out in parks in tents.

This scenario tells you about not only the emergency, it suggests what has been taken away. Implicitly we realize how efficient the freeway system normally is for the hundreds of thousands of cars that use it. We see in the ruins of the buildings details of the architecture we had not remarked before. We are reminded that schools run on a regular schedule. We note that these people in these makeshift dwellings have been shaken out of the ordinary patterns of their lives, and in contending with the loss of the ordinary patterns, we learn something of what those patterns were.

As I have in earlier chapters, I'm describing a premises-and-conclusions model, getting information across by implication. The audience thinks, "These people wouldn't be coping with the disruption in this way if their lives didn't ordinarily go this other way." The emergencies that we face have their roots in our normal lives. You aren't likely to rush your hamster to the pet hospital unless you have a hamster in the first place.

But then, plays and movies are not about the normal or everyday. They are about the special days, the unusual days—the days when the normal is disrupted and people's value systems are challenged and they have to improvise and adjust. And in the way they adjust they reveal to each other, the audience, and maybe themselves what they're really made of.

As I said above, one can also disrupt something as small as the expected pattern of words.

"If you can't say anything good about someone, don't say anything at all."

Odds are, once you read, "If you can't say anything good about someone," you probably gave a little mental "yeah, right, yawn" of impatience and skipped the rest of the line. The saying is a cliché. To use such a line is sleep-inducing. Here's how Washington socialite Alice Roosevelt Longworth subverted that line: "If you can't say something good about someone, sit right here by me." Such a twist subverts the cliché and sends a signal that the mind behind it is not content to pass along stale goods.

Dorothy Parker was known for such twists. In one of her book reviews, she wrote, "This is not a novel to be tossed aside lightly. It should be thrown aside with great force." The first sentence leads you to anticipate her urging you to take a second look at and give greater consideration to the book in question. The second line, of course, sabotages that anticipation completely.

Here's a reportedly true story that gets its punch line from an inversion:

A well-known and notoriously nasty Broadway leading man emerged from a stage door one day to encounter an adoring woman who wanted his autograph. The actor snarled, "Get out of my way," and shoved her so hard that the woman fell down onto the pavement. Whereupon the woman leapt to her feet and battered him with her umbrella. Commented an observer (I'm told it was Jonathan Miller)—"That's the first time I've seen a fan hit the shit."

Parodies, too, are based on the violation of expectation. Arthur Miller's *Death of a Salesman* contains a well-known scene in which Biff tells Willy that, after screwing up a job interview, he stole the interviewer's pen. In Second City's parody, Biff confesses to stealing the interviewer's desk. Simply by changing the size of the stolen object, the Second City players changed the whole tone of the scene.

The subversion of expected roles between characters can be a very useful tool. Remember Mr. Peabody of *The Rocky and Bullwinkle Show*? The joke of his relationship with the boy Sherman was that boys usually adopt dogs, but Mr. Peabody (being an unusually brilliant dog) adopted a boy. Simple inversion. This is not so different from Harold Pinter's screenplay of the Robin Maugham novel *The Servant*, in which the title character takes over the house from his employer.

I had fun violating a convention in *Responsible Parties*. A bully named A. J. Reese has been staying in a rundown motel owned by a man named Randolph. Randolph has been pressuring Reese to pay a substantial amount of back rent. One night, Reese shows up in a state of excitement with a wad of bills and offers them to Randolph, who is suspicious of their origin.

RANDOLPH: . . . . . Where'd you get the money?

    (A *beat.*)

REESE: Are you accusing me of something?

RANDOLPH: I'm asking to know where you got the money.

REESE: What difference does it make?

    (A *beat.*)

RANDOLPH: I'm not touching it.

REESE: I borrowed it.

RANDOLPH: Yeah? From who?

REESE: I've got friends.

RANDOLPH: Oh, friends give you the money?

REESE: Not give, they didn't *give.*

RANDOLPH: No?

REESE: They loaned.

RANDOLPH: They loaned you money?

REESE: They're friends.

RANDOLPH: Who are these friends?

REESE: What, you want names, addresses?

RANDOLPH: What I want is to know where you got it before I touch it.

REESE: You think it's contagious?

RANDOLPH: Are you going to tell me?

REESE: I told you.

RANDOLPH: You told me shit.

REESE: I don't have to take that from—

RANDOLPII. You stole it, didn't you?

REESE: No.

RANDOLPH: Then where'd you get it?

REESE: I don't have to tell you.

RANDOLPH: And I don't have to take the money.

REESE: Why don't you make it easy on both of us and just—just take it, OK?

RANDOLPH: I'm not touching it.

REESE: Can't you ease up this one time?

RANDOLPH: Not on your life.

(A *beat. Reese pulls out a pistol.*)

REESE: Take the money.

I tried to create sufficient momentum between the two belligerent men so that it would be credible that Reese lose what little judgment he has and pull the gun. The fun of writing this sequence was in subverting the convention of people being robbed at gunpoint. I don't know of any other scene in which a crook tries to compel someone to *take* money at gunpoint.

Of course, I didn't subvert convention merely for the technical pleasure of it. If I have written this scene correctly, this technique is in the service of making Reese a more vivid character, true to his own odd logic.

> **Assignment Twelve:** Focus on an expected pattern of behavior and, in the course of a scene between two people, violate that expectation.

By Susan B. Katz

(*Two painters sit on a scaffolding two stories up, over the front entryway to the First Methodist Church. The one on the left, Frank, is older than the one on the right by anywhere from 20 to 40 years. The one on the right is Kyle. Kyle paints some of the trim on the outside window. Frank leans over to inspect it.*)

FRANK: You can't do that. You just can't do that.

(*Kyle pauses.*)

Didn't they teach you anything at that school of yours? We're just gonna have to paint it again, you do that.

KYLE: I'm being careful.

FRANK: Nobody can be careful enough to paint without masking tape.[1]

KYLE: I can.

FRANK: No masking tape, you'll get smudges on there big as Virginia. We'll be stuck here till tomorrow cleaning up after your mess.

KYLE: Have you seen? Have you even seen? I've been painting this facade all morning and not once have I made a smudge.

FRANK: I seen you.[2] You don't even know what a smudge is. You wouldn't even recognize one if it came up and bit you on your Sherwin-Williams.

KYLE: Find it, then. I dare you find a smudge.

FRANK: I don't need to see. I know without looking you got smudges. It's the law of gravity. Paint don't stay where it's s'pozed to unless you got masking tape.

KYLE: Point to it. Show me. You show me a smudge and I'll buy you lunch.

FRANK: I got my lunch.

KYLE: A real lunch.

FRANK: Don't you go calling my Delores's lunch not a real lunch.

KYLE: At a restaurant.

FRANK: A real restaurant?

KYLE: You name it.

FRANK: The Two Swans.

KYLE: I was thinking more like Lucy's.

FRANK: I was thinking more like real.

KYLE: Lucy's, and you can get a combo plate, not just the enchiladas.

FRANK: You're small-time, Keel.

KYLE: Those plates are big, the combos.

FRANK: You make a bet, you make it a good one.[3]

KYLE: I am good.

FRANK: What do you know about good, holed up there in Yankeeland all winter long, coming down here just to party all sum-mer and grab a few bucks when you can, a few bucks from people who'd rather have those jobs and who would've done good work and known without me saying it he had to use masking tape.[4]

KYLE: Bet?

FRANK: Combo plate *and* a drink?

KYLE: And a drink.

FRANK: Jumbo drink?

KYLE: Forget it, then.

FRANK: No, no, I'm coming over.

> (*He gets up to walk across. As he walks, he jiggles the scaffolding a bit.*)

KYLE: Hey!

FRANK: Scared ya, didn't I? God, you'd think they'd have gotten one who'd gotten over his pansy fear of heights.[5]

KYLE: Look at it.

FRANK: I'm lookin', I'm lookin'.

> (*He peers at the window Kyle has just painted. He peers at it a second time, then reaches out to touch the part where there is no paint. He slowly turns and walks back over to his spot.*)

Poulet sauté Marengo.

KYLE: Pardon?

FRANK: Poulet sauté Marengo. Don't tell me you never had it.

KYLE: Can't say as I have.

FRANK: It's the best thing on the lunch menu at the Two Swans.

KYLE: Oh, no. I was talking Lucy's.

FRANK: I know you was talking Lucy's. I'm talking Two Swans, and that's what I'm gonna buy you for lunch.[6] Anybody can paint a window like that, a hand so steady he don't need masking tape . . . that's somebody who deserves poulet sauté Marengo—chicken, freshly wrung and plucked this morning—from a restaurant worthy of a paint job like that.

KYLE: You putting me on?

FRANK: Do I look like I would be putting you on, at twelve noon on the dot when I had breakfast at seven A.M.?

KYLE: What'd you have for breakfast?

FRANK: Delores made it. Poached eggs and grits. She's trying to cut down on my fats.

KYLE: Bacon?

(Frank shakes his head.)

FRANK: Cutting down on fats, I said. What'd you have?

KYLE: Grits and eggs.

(Pause.)

Sunny-side up. Salted, peppered.

FRANK: Yoke break? Mash it up real good in the grits?

(Kyle nods.)

It's the only way to go.[7]

(He turns to climb down the scaffold. Kyle follows.)

1. And here's our violation of convention: Kyle is doing the job differently than Frank is used to doing it, and this suggests that other differences exist between the two men.

2. When we write a scene, I think there always have to be answers to the questions, "Why now?" and "Why here?" The audience should get the impression that this stuff is happening between these people now and here because it couldn't happen any other time or elsewhere. This lends the action urgency and specificity.

   I don't have a "Why here?" problem with this piece. This action is organic to the work they are doing on the scaffolding.

   I do have a "Why now?" problem. If Frank has seen Kyle working in this manner all morning, what makes him raise the issue at this moment? Why has he waited all these hours to object? As a member of the audience, I suspect that he's raising the issue now because the lights on the stage just went up. That this occurs to me has the effect of undermining my belief in the scene. It may suit the author's purpose to have this topic arise now because the lights just came up, but Kyle and Frank don't know they're in a scene, so it's not a good reason for *them* to start dealing with this now. They must have their own reason—a reason organic to the scene—to address this particular issue at this particular time.

3. This negotiation over the bet, particularly over the restaurants, is persuasive. Without you explaining it, we get a sense of which is the more expensive place. We also get a sense that eating out is something that they are not in an economic position to do much, much less at the Two Swans.

4. For my taste, this passage is too overtly explanatory. I become aware of the effort of the writer to get information to me in the audience rather than believing that Frank is articulating these things to Kyle at this moment for an immediate purpose.

5. "Scared ya, didn't I?" works fine. I think the rest of the line is unnecessary. It articulates an attitude that's been implicit in Frank's behavior all along.

6. Getting to Frank's concession through the dish he's going to buy Kyle is very elegant. I think it's so elegant that the rest of the line, again, is unnecessary. Frank's respect is implicit in the dish he's promising to buy Kyle, it doesn't have to be articulated. It also has the effect of our transforming our opinion of him. He turns out to be an honorable guy, in spite of his bluffness, and that's a happy surprise.

7. The final chunk of this scene—the conversation about breakfast—is a nice application of the different voices idea from Lesson 8. Frank's tone has changed, as has Kyle's. These two guys who began as antagonists are now speaking like colleagues. As I said in earlier comments, a scene will move till the characters reach their true voices, or at least their true voices at this point in the story. The action of this scene is of two guys finding their true voices.

As has been the case with a number of other scenes, this piece works best when it deals with immediate and concrete actions and choices, and it tends to run into trouble when explanations for the audience's benefit are shoehorned in, or when characters articulate matter that the audience already has figured out for itself. Kyle's violating Frank's protocol for painting is an effective way to suggest their differences. Aside from answering the "Why now?" question, mostly what I think this scene needs to be as good as it could is some judicious pruning of the unmotivated and unnecessary.

By Lloyd Myoungwon Suh

(A streetside, curb, with window facing the audience. The lights are off. Paco enters, with flowers in his hand. Looks up at the window, sighs.)

PACO: Sofia!

(He throws a small rock. It hits the window.)

Sofia!

(A light from inside. Pause. Sofia opens the window. She is dressed in pajamas, and is beautiful. She hangs her hands over the windowsill.)[1]

SOFIA: Who's there?

PACO: It's me, Paco!

SOFIA: Paco . . . ! What are you doing?

PACO: I've come to serenade you.

(Sofia giggles. Paco digs into his pocket and takes out a scrap of paper.)

SOFIA: You plan to serenade me without a guitar?

PACO: I plan to serenade you with words.

SOFIA: Really . . . !

PACO *(Brandishing his scrap of paper)*: With poetry!

SOFIA: Oh, Paco . . .

(Pointing.)

And flowers . . . ?

PACO: Yes. I got them at the market. Lilies of the valley.

SOFIA: Oh, my very favorite flower.

PACO: I know.[2]

SOFIA: Paco, what is that you're wearing? You look so . . .

PACO: What?

SOFIA: So handsome.

PACO: You make me shiver when you say that, Sofia.

SOFIA: Shall I come down?

PACO: Yes. I mean no. Not until I've serenaded you.

SOFIA *(Giggling)*: Oh, Paco.

(She sits in the windowsill and leans.)

PACO: You're so beautiful.

SOFIA: And I am all yours for serenading.

PACO: I've written you a poem.

SOFIA: Ah. No man has ever written me a poem before.

PACO: Oh, but they have. I have seen them; hundreds of men, inspired by just a simple glance. When they pass by this window, they retreat to their homes, lock themselves away so they may compose endless poems, all for the love of Sofia. You simply have not heard these poems, but they exist. For their authors dare not speak them before you.[3]

SOFIA: Really.

PACO: Yep.

SOFIA: But you . . . you dare to read your poem to me?

PACO: I do.

SOFIA: What a brave and worthy man you must be.

PACO: There is none braver. And as for worth, my sweet Sofia, never could there be a man worthy of your loving glance.

SOFIA: Charmer.

(A beat. He laughs.)

Read to me.

PACO *(Reading)*: "My sweet Sofia, you who in passion and glory do illuminate the frosted, pale moon . . . ! May I drink from your sweet bosom the honey nectar wonder of your fullest and sweetest taste. Your lips, they are a juicy candy, which the shiver in my spine calls its mother. Your hands as delicate as an autumn night. Your hair as magnificent as a dance through the heavens, which is where you live, sweet Sofia, through all your beautiful days, now and forever."

(Pause. Sofia just looks at him.)

That's it.

SOFIA: Oh, it is?

PACO: You didn't like it.

SOFIA: Well, the part about the juicy candy I thought was a little strange.[4] And it's not always a good idea to talk about people's mothers. It doesn't exactly get the blood pumping.

PACO: Oh, but that . . . no, see, that was a *metaphor* . . .

SOFIA: I know what a metaphor is, like in the bit where you described the heavens as where I live, which just didn't make a whole lot of sense to me, because it almost gives the impression that, you know, if I live in heaven then—

PACO: If you didn't like the poem, I could try to remember the other one . . .

SOFIA: I think maybe you have a problem with adjectives.[5] Sometimes if you have too many descriptive phrases hinging on a single noun, like "honey nectar wonder," then you lose some of the specificity, not to mention the relevance.

PACO: I think I remember the other one . . . it's much better, actually, in fact it's the one that I—

SOFIA: And the line about the pale, frosted moon—I mean, did you mean for the verb to fractate the sentence that unevenly?[6] Because I think it might have served the expression more concisely if—

PACO: "Oh, moon! Savage and wild! How can you" . . . um. Wait. Hold on, no . . . that's not it.

SOFIA: And the imagery, see. I mean, if you're going to talk about the moon *and* the heavens, then you run the risk of mixing the metaphor, especially if one of them has to do with my hair and the other with electricity.

PACO: But . . .

SOFIA: I mean, don't get me wrong. There's a real spirit to the piece, which is nice and all. I just think if you paid more attention to syntax, you might see the ways you could guide that spirit into a tighter structure. Personally, I think it could help. There's actually a good text on the subject. I think it's Strunk and White, *The Elements of Style*.[7] I have a copy if you'd like. I could throw it down to you . . .

(*She goes into the room again, begins to search around, calling out.*)

It's around here somewhere.

PACO (*Shouting*): "Oh, moon! Wild and savage . . . !" Yeah, that's it. I mean, no . . .

> (*Sofia appears at the window again.*)

SOFIA: And see, that's just not right.

PACO: I mean, "Oh, savage moon!"

> (*Pause.*)

Aren't you going to come down?

SOFIA: Um.[8]

PACO: Flowers . . . ! I have lilies of the valley, they're, um—

SOFIA: I'm sorry, Paco.

> (*She goes back inside. The light goes out.*)

PACO: They're your favorite.

> (*Blackout.*)

1. Instantly we have in mind a pattern of behavior, informed by memories of *Romeo and Juliet* and *Cyrano*—the courtship of a fair lady by a suitor who appears below her window. Our expectations are set.

2. So far, everything is in place. Paco is making the appropriate romantic gestures and Sofia is expressing proper appreciation.

3. A beguiling introductory speech, further reinforcing the romantic patterns. Her reactions so far have confirmed her receptiveness to his overtures.

4. Uh-ohh, first sign that this may be a little bumpy.

5. Why do I feel as if I'm getting nudged?

6. As she moves into the specifics of the structure of his grammar, her voice changes from the would-be lover to something appropriate to a graduate teaching assistant working with an undergraduate.

7. Nice introduction of an object. He offers her flowers, she offers him a book on how to write well. The contrast is instructive.

8. A minute or so ago, she was eager to come down. Now she has changed her mind. We are now welcome to speculate as to what has happened in the meantime to motivate this change.

This scene addresses the assignment of violating an expected pattern by invoking a romantic image, and then having our (and his) expectations of what is to follow be upended by her qualms about his writing ability. This is also a good example of the roles-in-conflict scene: her role as a lady willing to be wooed is in conflict with a woman whose intellect is clearly superior to her would-be lover's. Ultimately, she cannot subordinate her intelligence to her passions.

13

LESSON

Violation of Settings

EVERY LOCATION HAS ITS OWN CHARACTER. EVERY LOCATION—
particularly if it has been designed by an architect, interior decorator, land-
scaper, or any of the others who make their livings by tinkering with space—
has implicit in its layout its own code telling you how to behave there.

Edward T. Hall (whom I mentioned before) brings this up in his book,
The Hidden Dimension. He says, for example, that when you go into an airport waiting area, the people who designed that area did so in order to
give you only so much comfort. They don't want you hanging around.
They bolt the seats side by side so that conversation between groups of
people is difficult. The people managing traffic control at the airport don't
want you to feel too welcome there. They want to motivate you to keep
moving. This becomes particularly relevant on days when you *can't* keep
moving, such as during the annual blizzard when a lot of people get stuck
there for hours, waiting for their flights in irritation and discomfort. The
airports were not *designed* to accommodate them for that long. (This is one
of the secrets behind the various clubs the airlines have created for frequent travelers. I had a coupon to go into Continental's President's Club
in Newark a couple of years ago. This place has everything the regular
waiting area doesn't—attractive lighting, comfortable chairs and
couches, places to plug in your computer, free coffee, plentiful newspa-
pers, and a bar. One of the incentives to join the President's Club is the
desire frequent travellers have to escape the uncomfortable places their
designers designed to be uncomfortable.)

Hall also says that when you go to a movie theatre, the space obviously gives you instructions. You have only limited options regarding seating, and, of course, the seats point you in the direction of where the film is going to be projected.

Determinists believe that environment helps shape behavior and character. They say that if you are in an ordered world, you will be encouraged to be orderly. You probably notice your own behavior is a bit different when you're in a Burger King, say, than when you're in a fancy, expensive restaurant like the Four Seasons. Or when you go to a sports bar or one of those Sunday buffets in a hotel's restaurant where there are thirty thousand options for stuffing yourself.

Some spaces are earmarked for professional behavior as opposed to personal behavior. You know what is appropriate behavior in a dentist's office and that it is different than the behavior you would expect in a bedroom. If the dentist in question were having an affair in the office after hours, suddenly the professional space would be adapted (and probably with funny results) to accommodate bedroom activity. (Of course, this is just a hypothetic example. I'm sure such things never happen.)

Or, say, using a personal space as a professional space. This is one of the things that's amusing and wrenching about watching people be interviewed for TV in their homes. Private spaces—Robin Williams' living room, say—suddenly become semipublic with the addition of lights and cords and microphones and whatnot. (In fact, a lot of stars won't let anybody but Barbara Walters come into their homes. Many of these taped interviews are done in hotels now, precisely because the stars don't want their private spaces violated by public exposure or turned into temporary TV studios.)

The violation of space may also involve using an environment against its designed status. Take, for example, an opera house. The term brings to mind an elegantly dressed audience and decorous behavior (except onstage, where the characters are frequently slaughtering each other to great music). Now imagine some maniacs playing baseball in the orchestra pit. The Marx Brothers in A N*ight at the Opera*. A classic case of the use of a high-status location for a low-status activity. (The Marx Brothers didn't restrict this kind of behavior to their movies. They were once ushered into the office of Irving Thalberg for a scheduled appointment with the legendary movie producer. Thalberg arrived very late to find that the Marx Brothers had stripped naked and were toasting marshmallows over a campfire they had improvised in his office. Incidentally, Thalberg produced A Night at the Opera.)

A low-status location may also effectively host a high-status occasion. Where does the Bible tell us Jesus was born? In a manger. A structure meant to house animals (low status) is transformed into the birthplace of the son of God (can't get much higher status than that).

Assignment Thirteen: Come up with a location and write a short scene in which something occurs there that is out of character with this environment. Don't just go for Monty Python absurdity (like, say, holding a murder trial in a laundromat). Come up with reasons why this is happening here and now. You may well find that an "ordinary" scene you've set up plays with a special sparkle by transposing it to an unlikely place.

By Jamie Pachino

(Lily, 17, and Boggy, male, 18, an attractive, offbeat pair in a high school art class. Several [unseen] students surround them, working in pairs. An Art Teacher strolls through. Boggy and Lily paint wooden frames from pans of different-color paint in front of them. They work in silence a moment, then:)

BOGGY: What happened to the man refinishing the flagpole?

LILY: What?

BOGGY: He varnished into thin air.

(She laughs. The Art Teacher looks over. Lily paints, looking down. After a moment:)

Why were the two blood cells so unhappy?

LILY: . . . why?

BOGGY: They loved in vein.

LILY: Boggy . . .

BOGGY: What's the best way to talk to a monster?

LILY (*Laughing against her better judgment*): What?

BOGGY: Long distance![1]

    (*She laughs out loud, covers her mouth.*)

You should laugh more. You have a nice laugh.[2]

LILY: You don't know me that well.

BOGGY: You think I'm dorky. Because I like riddles?

LILY: No.

BOGGY: Immature?

LILY: No.

BOGGY: 'Cause you know, they're not all funny.

LILY: They're great.

BOGGY: Some are like—poetic, come from different countries, they're more—

LILY: Do one. Like that.

BOGGY: Okay. Okay . . . why is a man like a pepper?

LILY: Why?

BOGGY: 'Cause you don't know how strong he is till you've tested him. Want to hear another?

LILY: Sure.

BOGGY: What is it even a giraffe can't see?

LILY: I don't know.

BOGGY: What will happen tomorrow. How do you spot a leopard?

LILY: How?

BOGGY: You don't have to, they already come that way.

    (*She laughs. The Art Teacher snaps her fingers from across the room.*)

ART TEACHER: Focus, please.

    (*They work, looking down. Boggy smiles.*)

BOGGY: Caught you.

LILY (*Under*): You know, they call her the Dragon Lady. You should probably—

BOGGY: You don't have girl hands.

LILY: . . . What?

BOGGY: I've noticed.

LILY: You noticed my hands?

BOGGY: They're all roughed up. Like they've been used.

LILY: Like a car?

(*Boggy takes her hand.*)

BOGGY: Like a person. Most girls' hands don't look like they've done anything. I like things that are useful.[3] What if we mixed all these colors together? What do you think the Dragon would say then?

LILY (*Trying not to laugh*): She'd have a fit.

(*He takes his brush, loaded with paint, holds it up.*)[4]
No—no don't! You wouldn't.

(*He flings the paint off it into her tray.*)

BOGGY: You don't know me that well.

LILY (*Laughing, under*): She'll kill you.

(*Trying to do some damage control.*)
I may kill you.

(*He does it again. Picks up another color, tries another mix.*)

BOGGY: You rather I stick to the rules.

LILY: No! That's not true. I just—

BOGGY:—what?

LILY: It'll make a terrible color.

(*He laughs this time. The Art Teacher looks over, snaps her fingers, sharp.*)

ART TEACHER: Lily!

(*Pointing to Boggy.*)
You—! What's your name—new boy—[5]

BOGGY: Bogsworth Barry. But I prefer Boggy if you—

ART TEACHER: Pay attention to what you're doing.

BOGGY: Yes ma'am.

(*A silence. Lily smiles, satisfied.*)

LILY: Caught you.

BOGGY: Listen. Could I kiss you?

LILY: What?

BOGGY: I'd like to kiss you.

LILY: You mean right now?

BOGGY: Listen Lily. I held your hand. I made you laugh. You got me into trouble. Kissing comes next. Can I kiss you?

LILY: I—

> (*Looks around. Charmed by the daring of it, him.*)

. . . okay.

BOGGY: Okay.

> (*He does a short, funny preparation, moving in on her. The kiss is very caring, tender.*)[6]

LILY: That was nice.

BOGGY: That *was* nice. Can I—

ART TEACHER: Bobby!

BOGGY: Boggy.

ART TEACHER (*Not hearing*): Lily! The two of you—

> (*The school bell rings. The Art Teacher claps her hands, shouting over the students.*)

Clean up! No one leaves till we're—

> (*Lily starts to move. Boggy grabs one of her hands.*)

BOGGY: Wait.

> (*He reaches over, and dips her hand into one of the paint trays, and presses it into his T-shirt, leaving her handprint behind.*)[7]

You made a mark on me.

LILY (*Smiles, taken aback*): I could've just signed my name.

BOGGY: Handprints're better. I'd find you again from your hands. See?

> (*Looks at the handprints.*)

You Were Here.[8]

LILY: I've got to— I've got chemistry and—

> (*Looks at her hands, laughs.*)

BOGGY: Can I see you later? Like after school? Tonight? Sometime? Say yes.[9]

LILY: Yes. Okay.

BOGGY: Okay.

    (She starts to move away. Calling after her:)

Hey!

    (She turns.)

What's the most important thing to remember in chemistry?

LILY: What?

BOGGY: Don't lick the spoon!

    (Lily laughs.)

1. Without having it overtly articulated, we figure out that the Art Teacher is in a position of authority over Lily and Boggy and that Boggy is trying to win Lily's good opinion by clowning with her.

2. My opinion? You probably don't need, "You have a nice laugh." "You should laugh more" takes care of confirming that he likes the laugh.

3. The introduction of the "girl hands" idea nicely moves into the area of his attraction to her. "I like things that are useful" strikes me as being redundant; he's already said that he admires her hands because "they've been used." I'm being picky, but I think the audience has already reached this conclusion before he articulates it.

4. Here, again, the technique of the misuse, transformation, or destruction of objects (covered in Lesson 3) comes in handy. Of course, to do this with the paints is part of violating the setting of the art class.

5. The Art Teacher calling Boggy "new boy" is a nicely motivated piece of exposition. It helps establish that Boggy is indeed new to the class and so new, too, to Lisa.

6. Yes, kissing in a classroom, behind the back of a strict teacher, is forbidden and so all the more entertaining.

7. Lovely gesture. And, of course, it marks the transformation of his T-shirt and the beginning of the next step in the relationship.

8. The handprint moment is so charming and resonant that I think its power is diluted by his interpreting it for her. I think you could go straight from the making of the handprint to him saying, "Can I see you later?" and the audience's heart would stop in the interval.

9. I think this scene would end best right here, when he's asking to see her again and she hasn't made her decision. Bring the lights down now, and the audience will want to see the next scene to see what she decided.

By L. G. Watson

(Outdoors. The sound of crickets. Mary Ellen is sitting hunched on the ground. She's wearing a bathing suit with a terry cloth robe wrapped tightly over it, and sandals. Jack enters, hair wet, a towel around his waist.)

JACK: Hey Scooter.

(She is silent, ignores him.)

We were getting ready to send out a search party. You're not still mad, are you?

MARY ELLEN: A spa, you said. A "rustic resort."

JACK: Oh boy, here we go.

MARY ELLEN: "Todd and Ginger go up there all the time, they absolutely love it." I can't believe I am even socializing with people named Todd and Ginger, thank you very much.[1] Much less—

JACK: So we'll leave early, okay? Called away by, I don't know, a sick aunt.[2]

MARY ELLEN: And how are we going to get out of here? Seeing as we're not even in our own car? Jeez, what a mess.[3]

JACK: It's not that bad, you know. The hot pool *is* relaxing. Kind of soapy. The water holds you up.

MARY ELLEN: I'll pass, thanks.

JACK: And c'mon, smell the air. Incense cedars. It's beautiful country out here.

(He follows with his eyes as somebody walks past.)

MARY ELLEN: Yes, you can hardly keep your eyes off the scenery. God!

(She gets up.)

I'm going . . . I don't know where I'm going.

(She sits down again.)

JACK: Honey—calm down.

MARY ELLEN: This is Todd and Ginger's idea of relaxation? A nudist colony?[4]

JACK: It's a clothing-optional hot springs, Mary Ellen.

MARY ELLEN: It doesn't look freaking optional to me. I'm the only one in two square miles who doesn't have all her parts dangling out, thank you very much.[5]

JACK: I've seen a couple other bathing suits.

MARY ELLEN: Right, on the ten-year-old. Who in God's name takes their ten-year-old to a place like this?

JACK: Look, I said I was sorry.

MARY ELLEN: Did you notice that Ginger has a tattoo of a cartoon chipmunk on her right ass cheek?[6] I shouldn't have to know that about her.

JACK: So keep your clothes on.[7]

MARY ELLEN: You better believe I will. If I had packed a burnoose, I'd be wearing it right now.

JACK: Jeez, Scooter, I didn't think you'd be so bent out of shape.

MARY ELLEN: You didn't think.

JACK: I just . . . I don't see the big deal about it. I mean, you're hardly a prude.

MARY ELLEN: See, that's the problem, Jack. I've been sitting here for, what? an hour and forty-five minutes, trying to figure it out. Figure out what I'm doing engaged to a guy who would drag me into the bare-ass naked Northern California woods with his sales manager and bimbette girlfriend without letting me know what to expect.[8] Because I know damn well *you* knew what was up here.

JACK: I didn't—

MARY ELLEN: Yes you did! You did, don't deny it. And I, gullible pinhead that I am, walked right into it. So I've been thinking. Maybe I've been asking for it—

JACK: C'mon, Scooter.

MARY ELLEN:—the way I've always been such a "good sport," you know? Such a good girl that I wouldn't say boo if somebody served me leftover rubber tires, I'd just smile, pour ketchup on them, and saw away at them politely until they were done. How did I get to be like that? Is that the kind of wife I think I'm supposed to be?

(Pause.)

So what's the next test going to be? A little swap on a moonlit night? Or maybe a threesome with the silicone-enhanced Ginger?

(She takes off one of her sandals, throws it at him.)

JACK: Ow! Jesus, don't make a scene out here, Mary Ellen, I gotta work with the guy!

MARY ELLEN: No you don't. You do not have to work with the guy. It's a great market, find another job.

JACK: What—what the hell are you doing? This isn't like you![9]

(Mary Ellen throws another sandal at him.)

MARY ELLEN: Yes it is. It's exactly like me. I'm turning into the kind of wife I've decided I'm going to be. One who makes non-negotiable demands. One who makes a scene when faced with creepy, underhanded, unpalatable things.

Often this violation-of-setting technique is used to depict the violation of a conservative milieu, a place where propriety is violated. One of the things that tickles me about this scene is that it is a reversal of this pattern—here the setting is a place notable for its *lack* of conventional propriety and Mary Ellen is violating it by hewing to her personal sense of propriety and refusing to doff her duds. Additional thoughts:

1. Another instance of the dreaded "I can't believe—"

2. As is often true, moving to the future tense is an effective choice for heightening the immediacy of a scene. When people propose solutions, one gathers that there are indeed problems that need to be addressed.

3. "Jeez, what a mess" is an evaluation that you probably don't need. Her whole attitude conveys the idea that she thinks the situation is a mess, so having her say this simply reinforces what we already know.

4. Of course, the whole scene is predicated on the fact that they're in a nudist colony, which makes me wonder if there is any way to get this across without overtly announcing it. This is another instance in which I think it would be useful to leave the most important word(s) in the scene unsaid so that the audience can figure it out for themselves. Besides, I think in this case, having Mary Ellen say "nudist colony" falls under the heading of someone with a high-context relationship saying a low-context line. She knows that Jack knows what "this" she's talking about when she says, "This is Todd and Ginger's idea of relaxation?" So the only reason the words "a nudist colony" are in the scene is so that you, the author, can make the setting clear to the audience.

5. As I've mentioned before, it tends to be more effective if the most important word, phrase, or image in a line is at the end of the line. "Thank you very much" isn't the most important phrase in the line. I suggest that "parts dangling out" is and so would be more effective at the end.

6. Nice specific detail and one I think you might be able to use earlier in the scene to address the issue I raise in 4. "I shouldn't have to know that about her" establishes that they're in a specific setting where Mary Ellen would get to see the chipmunk. Between this detail and the fact that the scene is outdoors, we in the audience would put together the idea "nudist colony" for ourselves.

7. This line earlier would also make the overt reference to a nudist colony unnecessary. Where else would one be told it's OK to keep her clothes on?

8. This line sounds like the writer sneaking in exposition.

9. "What are you doing?" and "This isn't like you," are lines that the audience can finish before they're begun. They are functional and generic and they've been used in thousands of plays, which means that the ear goes a little dead when they're used. I think that whenever a character speaks, you have the opportunity to serve the moment with something fresh. What reaction could he have that would be specific to him?

14
LESSON

Characters Treated By

PART OF THURGOOD MARSHALL'S CASE IN BROWN V. BOARD OF *Education* was based on the idea that, by treating black students worse than white students, one sent a signal that was internalized by a black child: "I am being treated worse, so I must deserve to be treated worse." This crippled blacks' self-image and tended to set them on a path of self-fulfilling prophecy. Marshall's argument helped prompt the Supreme Court to make the historic decision that so-called separate-but-equal schools were inherently separate and unequal and so to order desegregation.

As Marshall insisted, we learn much of who we are by looking in the mirrors of other people's eyes. If I walk into a room and am instantly surrounded by a cheering throng, and someone raises a champagne glass and makes a toast to me in which all and sundry enthusiastically join, I'm probably going to feel good about myself. On the other hand, if I enter a room and, after looking at me with disdain, all and sundry head for the exits, my self-esteem is going to take a dive. Identity is not only what we carry around with us. It is what we confer on each other.

So, too, with a character. The audience will evaluate a figure we place onstage at least in part by watching how the others on the stage deal with that person or the presence of that person in their lives.

If big burly guys bow and scrape to a small Italian woman, even without anybody overtly articulating the reasons, we get the idea that she has a good deal of power or somehow commands respect.

If, in a pickup bar, the tall, very good-looking guy can't get any of the attractive women in the bar to talk to him while short, balding guys with glasses are making out like crazy, we'll get some idea of the lack of esteem in which the good-looking guy is held.

I once saw a college production of A *Funny Thing Happened on the Way to the Forum* in which, because of an injured actor, the director had to play the captain, Miles Gloriosus. The captain is usually played by a towering figure with rippling muscles—the image of an egocentric bully. The director of this production, however, was scrawny in the Arnold Stang–Wally Cox mode. Still, because he was playing the bullying captain, everyone onstage shook in their shoes whenever he strode into view. They may have been looking down when they shook, but they shook. This was wonderfully funny, because what they were reacting to was not his *size* (or his physical ability to dominate the others, which is the usual thing) but his *role*.

It is even possible to characterize people without their being onstage. Two of the most vivid characters in dramatic literature enter fairly late in the plays they dominate—Walter Burns, the s.o.b. editor in Ben Hecht and Charles MacArthur's *The Front Page*, makes his physical entrance at the end of the second act of a three-act play. But by then he's already been characterized. When reporter Hildy Johnson abuses him over the phone, the other reporters in the room gasp at his guts. Clearly Burns is not the sort of man to whom one speaks in this way with any expectation of living. The reporters' reaction to Hildy's treatment of Burns indirectly but very vividly gives us an impression of how formidable Burns is.

Tartuffe enters in the third act of the five-act Molière play that bears his name, but again we have a strong sense of who he is by how his presence in the household (offstage) affects the behavior of the characters onstage in those first two acts.

A. R. Gurney built his play *Children* on the device of an unseen character. The piece concerns a woman's relationship to her three grown children and their significant others. Two of the children and the wife of one appear onstage. The third, a son nicknamed Pokey, never actually appears onstage (though his shadow is seen outlined behind a screen door late in the script), yet the play is largely about the effect of his visit on the rest of the family. The others discuss the choices and challenges he is setting before them, and through the agitation he causes we get a sense of how troubled and moody he is. Pokey is as vividly characterized by Gurney as the four characters we do see.

As I mentioned in an earlier chapter, *The Value of Names* builds to a confrontation between Benny Silverman and Leo Greshan, the man who betrayed him by naming his name to H.U.A.C. years before. I wanted to establish something of Leo's character sometime before he actually made his entrance, so I wrote the following scene between Benny and his actress daughter Norma.

NORMA: There was another book I found, on political theatre. And there was a picture. A photo of the Labor Players—

BENNY (*Correcting*): The *New* Labor Players.

NORMA: Maybe seven or eight of you in the picture. And standing next to you is Leo Greshen, and your arm is around his shoulder.

BENNY: That was a fake arm. They touched that arm into the picture.

NORMA: He was a friend of yours.

BENNY: He gave that appearance for a while.

NORMA: So what did he say?

BENNY: Look it up. The transcript's public, it's easy to find.

NORMA: I don't mean his testimony. I mean what did he say to you?

BENNY: Why you want to dig into this is beyond—

NORMA: Did he call you afterwards? Try to explain?

BENNY: Not afterwards, before. Squealer's etiquette. Sort of like an arsonist calling up ahead of time. "Hello, I'm going to burn your house down. Thought you might like to know." Only instead—"Hello, I'm going to burn your career down." "Thanks a lot, Leo. Hope to return the favor someday."

NORMA: But he was a friend. Didn't he give you reasons?

BENNY: Oh, everybody knew the reasons why. He had the prospect of directing his first picture, and he didn't want this to blow it for him.

NORMA: He said this to you? That was why he was going to testify?

BENNY: Did you know "testify" and "testimony" come from the same Latin root as "testes" as in "balls"? I'm not making this up. In Rome, if you wanted to make a big point that something you said was true, when you said it, you'd grab your balls. Which is why I don't think what he said to the Committee really qualifies as testimony. How could it? The man had no balls to grab.

> **Assignment Fourteen:** Write a scene in which you characterize a character primarily by the way the other people onstage treat that character or behave because that character is present in their lives. You can choose to either have that character onstage or off. But, if onstage, the character should do and say very little. The whole point of the assignment is to dramatize him or her through the behavior of the others.

By *Michael Ladenson*

(*Living room. Phil Goldstone, in a suit, is talking with Mrs. Gibson.*)

MRS. GIBSON: No. I'm sorry, Mister, but I will not treat my Willie like a criminal.

GOLDSTONE: We don't look at it that way, Ma'am.

MRS. GIBSON: Well, what other way is there to look at it? In my time, a coupla kids were horsing around in the hall, ya boxed their ears, made 'em stay after school. You didn't call the coppers in to search their car.[1]

GOLDSTONE: Your son threatened to kill the Richman girl.[2]

MRS. GIBSON: Oh, fiddlesticks.[3]

GOLDSTONE: Ma'am, we have witnesses—

MRS. GIBSON: I know my boy, I know the difference between when he's foolin' around and when he's serious. And if that girl wants to get anywhere with the boys, and which one doesn't, then she better find out, too. Little b-i-t-c-h if you ask me.

GOLDSTONE: Mrs. Gibson, I'm sure this is very difficult for you.

MRS. GIBSON: Mr. Goldstein—

GOLDSTONE: Gold*stone*, Mrs. Gibson.

MRS. GIBSON: These days, ya can't even—well, anyway, Mr.

Gold*stone*, I've found that the kids can usually settle it among themselves, without our interference.

GOLDSTONE: Some of the kids have *asked* us to interfere. And not just girls—boys, too.

MRS. GIBSON: We used to have a word for those kind of boys.

GOLDSTONE: I know, William still uses it.

MRS. GIBSON: Mister, my Willie doesn't have a father. He's lonely! He's very anxious for people to like him. So he clowns around, maybe goes a little far sometimes. He needs a helping hand, not a kick in the boot!

(Goldstone pulls out a form and a pen.)

GOLDSTONE: Ma'am, if you're right, then taking a look into his car won't hurt at all. If there's no more Nazi paraphernalia—

MRS. GIBSON: Oh, Lord!

GOLDSTONE: And no more inappropriate material, if he hasn't brought a gun onto school grounds, then he gets a clean bill of health, there's no trouble and everyone can breathe easier.

MRS. GIBSON: I just don't think there's any point to grown men running around hysterical like little sissy boys at ballet class. And I don't see any reason—

GOLDSTONE: Mrs. Gibson, we are going to search Willie's car. Now, if we have to bring in the police, then so be it. We thought we could avoid that. We think it would be better for him, and better for you, to avoid a police warrant. And, of course, much easier for us.

(Checks watch.)

Look—it's two-thirty now. His last class finishes in half an hour—

MRS. GIBSON: It's *what*?[4] Oh, dear.

(She gets up hurriedly.)

Listen, sonny, I hate to be rude, but I have to go.

GOLDSTONE: I'm afraid we're not done yet, ma'am.

MRS. GIBSON: Didn't you hear me? I have to go to the store. Now don't give Mama any trouble, just run along, please.

GOLDSTONE: I'm sorry, I can't do that.

MRS. GIBSON: You—what do you mean?[5] You have to go! I need to get to the store, I have to leave now! Come on!

GOLDSTONE: Not till I have your signature on that paper and the keys in my hand, ma'am.

MRS. GIBSON: Oh, shoot shoot sugar! Just a second!

    (Picks up phone and presses speed dial; the tones beep quickly.)

Elsie? Yes, it's May Gibson, now listen—

GOLDSTONE: Mrs. Gibson—

    (She waves him to be quiet.)

MRS. GIBSON: I need you to do me a little favor, it's very, very important. Yes, now! Go to the 7-Eleven on Forster and get two packages of Suzy-Q's.

    (A beat.)

It's a snack, you know, like Ring Dings. No, don't get Ring Dings, you have to get Suzy-Q's! The chocolate ones. If they have another flavor, make sure you get chocolate!

GOLDSTONE: Ma'am—

MRS GIBSON *(To him)*: Please!

    (Into phone.)

Elsie, I need you to do it now. *Now.* Before three o'clock. And bring them here. You've got to get them here by three!

    (A beat.)

Never mind, just do it, please. Please, Elsie! Two packs. All right? Thank you.[6]

    (Hangs up.)

GOLDSTONE: He likes his snack, does he?

MRS. GIBSON: I don't know why everything has to be such a G. D. *rigmarole.*

GOLDSTONE: I'm sorry, Mrs. Gibson. If you would just sign that paper and hand me the keys, I'd be out of your hair in a snap. We're not talking about fooling around in school, we're talking about a boy who is known to own guns, to be proficient with guns—

MRS. GIBSON: Oh, this is such a rigmarole, too, and I'm tired of it. Willie's no different than any boy here, he knows how to use his rifle and his pistol like a responsible fellow—[7]

GOLDSTONE: He has a pistol?

(*Mrs. Gibson's hand instinctively goes to her mouth. Pause.*) I think I'll be going now, ma'am.

MRS. GIBSON: Wait—

(*Goldstone puts away his form and pen.*)

GOLDSTONE: I don't think there's much chance of keeping the police out of this now, Mrs Gibson.

MRS. GIBSON: Hold on—

GOLDSTONE: We're going to have to ask him to surrender that pistol, Mrs.—

MRS. GIBSON: YOU CAN'T ASK HIM ABOUT THE PISTOL.

(*Pause.*)

What I mean is, if you ask him about that pistol, if you mention anything at all about that pistol, he's going to know where you got the information.

GOLDSTONE: I don't think there's any way we can avoid it, ma'am.

MRS. GIBSON: Mr. Goldstone, I am all alone here. You cannot ask him about that pistol.

(*Pause.*)

Please.[8]

GOLDSTONE: The situation seems to have changed, then.

MRS. GIBSON: Don't take cheap shots at me, Mr. Goldstone.[9] What do I have to do?

(*He takes out his form, and puts in on the table, with a pen.*)

GOLDSTONE: We can have that car open before he even gets out of class.

(*Mrs. Gibson crosses to her purse, takes out a key ring and removes a key. She hesitates.*)

MRS. GIBSON: Won't he know I gave permission?

GOLDSTONE: If we find anything very inappropriate, they can take him into juvenile custody immediately.

(Mrs. Gibson hands him the key and signs the paper.)

MRS. GIBSON: That opens the car and the trunk both.

GOLDSTONE: Thank you, Mrs. Gibson.

(He takes the paper and pen, starts to leave.)

MRS. GIBSON: Mr. Goldstone.

(He stops.)

If you take him to that place—

GOLDSTONE:—yes?

MRS. GIBSON: Then you better know how to keep him there.[10]

GOLDSTONE: We'll try, ma'am.

(He goes. She sits, staring as lights fade.)

1. My hunch is that you can start this scene at, "In my time, a coupla kids . . ." The ideas you introduce in the earlier lines will be in implicit in the action of the rest of the scene.

2. I think this line might be more effective if either it were more vague ("He threatened the Richman girl") or more specific ("He threatened to come after the Richman girl with a knife"). This is probably a matter of personal taste.

3. The words "coppers" and "fiddlesticks" suggest an archaic vocabulary in the employ of someone whose language has not made peace with the present and, perhaps, works actively to deny the present. Now that I think of it, I can't remember the word "coppers" being used since Jimmy Cagney. I wonder if this might undermine some viewers' belief in this character?

4. Mrs. Gibson's "It's *what*?" is a response to Goldstone saying, "Look—it's two-thirty now." But between his line and her response, Goldstone says, "His last class finishes in half an hour—" her response seems to be unnaturally delayed. Ordinarily, the catalyst and the response should be closer together. My suggestion would be

   GOLDSTONE: Look—it's two-thirty now.
   MRS. GIBSON: It's *what*? Oh, dear.

GOLDSTONE: His last class finishes in half an hour—

MRS. GIBSON: Oh, dear.

5. I'm not a fan of the line, "What do you mean?" Most of the times, it either is a cue for an overt explanation (which, as I've explained, I find undramatic) or it is unnecessary. I think if you cut "What do you mean?" here, the result would be effective.

6. We get the idea here that the urgency with which she recruits Elsie to get the Suzy-Q's is related to the imminent arrival of her son, which suggests that things may be difficult for her if the boy returns and finds that the Suzy-Q's aren't there. This is the first hint of how afraid she is of him.

7. Her use of the phrase "responsible fellow" doesn't sound like credible American speech to my ear; more like something out of a Dickens novel.

8. Now her fear of her son becomes even more apparent. This is all done by suggestion. There is nothing concrete said about what actions he would be likely to take, just that whatever they might be, she has cause to fear them.

9. As I've mentioned before, lines in which people evaluate the lines of others frequently strike me as being unnecessary. The audience usually has arrived at the evaluation already. I think you could just go straight to her "What do I have to do?" The speed of her capitulation would be arresting and telling. Besides, "Don't take cheap shots at me," doesn't sound consistent with the rather quaint language she uses in a lot of the scene.

10. I think this last line is a stronger one than having Goldstone reply to her. The look he gives her as she says this will carry more dramatic weight than anything he could say.

I don't know what legal mechanism is involved in looking in the car. If you made it clear that she held title to the car but he used it, then probably all he would need is her verbal permission. My hunch also is that he would ask her to open the trunk of the car rather than taking her keys.

Much of the information that people get about the way society works is stuff they glean from dramatic forms. I think this gives those of us who write scripts a particular responsibility to present these matters as accurately as possible, and this includes getting the procedures right. If this means doing some research, then so be it: do the research into the way this sort of thing is really handled. In the course of doing the research, you'll be likely to come up with some unexpected detail you can include that will add to the piece's specificity and credibility.

By Genuine Crystal

Some Bitch Named Veronica

(Girls' bathroom in a school. Janey and Katora are standing at the bathroom mirror. They are dressed for a dance.)

JANEY: Did you see her?

KATORA: No, which one is she?

JANEY: The one with the long hair, in the tight dress.

KATORA: Wavy, black hair?

JANEY: No blonde. Kinda reddish. She probably dyed it to match that short, skimpy thing she's wearing.[1]

(Juanita and Marla enter.)

JUANITA: Janey! What's up, girl?

JANEY: Hey Juanita, Maria. This is my cousin, Katora.

JUANITA: Hey, Katora.

MARLA: Hi, Katora.

KATORA: Hi.

JUANITA: Where do you go, Katora?

KATORA: Kennedy.[2]

JUANITA: You know Mark Greene?

KATORA: No.

JANEY: What's she doin' out there?

JUANITA: Dancin'.

JANEY: With who?

JUANITA: Everybody.[3]

KATORA: Was she the one with the puffy thing on her arm?

JUANITA: Puffy thing on her arm?

MARLA: No, I know who you're talking about. That's not her.

JUANITA: You can't miss her. She's got this hair that's all over the place, and she has this bright orange, Day-Glo fluorescent, neon, traffic-sign color dress on.

MARLA: Does Dory know she's here?

JUANITA: Somebody should call her.[4]

JANEY: She's not home.

JUANITA: Then let's page her.

JANEY: I'm gonna call her when I get home. She told me to give her the full report.

JUANITA: When did you talk to her? In school?

JANEY: No. She called me right before she left to go out.

JUANITA: So she going with the—

    (Taylor enters.)

MARLA (*In a singsong voice*): Taylor!

TAYLOR: Hey, girls. What's going on?

JANEY: What's she doin' now?[5]

TAYLOR: Who? That skank? Getting some punch or something stupid like that.

JUANITA: Some punch?

TAYLOR: Yeah. She standing around the snack table laughing at everybody's corny jokes like it's Comic View or something.

JUANITA: Oh.

JANEY: She is so phony.

MARLA: She's lucky Dory isn't here.

KATORA: I still don't know which one she is. She has real long hair?

TAYLOR: It's like a strawberry blonde color.

MARLA: It's a weave.

KATORA: Was she—

JUANITA: You must not have seen her. You would have remembered. Do you know Greg Phillips?

KATORA: I think I do.

JUANITA: He hangs around with Mark. Okay, Mark's brother goes there, too. Do you know any other Greenes at your school?

TAYLOR: Who's she talking about?

JANEY: Some guy she's trying to kick it to.

TAYLOR: Why's she—

(Door opens. In walks Veronica. All stop and stare at her. She glances in the mirror, then turns to go into a stall. All the other girls rush past her into the four stalls. Janey pulls Katora into handicapped stall with her.[6] Veronica waits outside for a moment, then becomes impatient.)

VERONICA: Could one of you come out, please? I need to use the bathroom.

(No one responds.)

Would you hurry up, it's kind of an emergency.

(Some snickering can be heard from within the stalls. Veronica bangs on the door.)

Come on! Open the door!

(Veronica continues to talk, but her voice is drowned out by sound of simultaneous toilet flushing.[7] She keeps pushing on doors until one finally opens. Marla stands blocking her entrance.)

MARLA: Hey, she got one opened!

(Juanita comes out.)

JUANITA: Which one?

(Veronica rushes to toward the stall Juanita has just left, but as more girls come out of stalls they block her entrance and begin to force her backwards towards the wall.)

VERNOICA: Move! Leave me alone!

ALL EXCEPT KATORA: Bitch! Bitch!

(They continue to taunt her while Katora watches, stunned. Eventually they block her into a corner. Finally she breaks away and runs out the door. They disburse laughing and falling over each other.)[8]

MARLA (*Laughing hysterically*): She peed in her pants!

KATORA: What?

MARLA (*Still laughing*): She peed in her pants!

(*Taylor exits, laughing.*)

KATORA: Why did you all do that to her?

MARLA: Because she's a bitch.

KATORA: But what did she do?

JUANITA: She did everybody! She's a ho.

KATORA: Janey, why are you guys being so mean?

JANEY: That's the girl that's messing with Dory's man.

JUANITA: Dory's ex.

KATORA: You mean Dory's not even with him anymore?

JUANITA: Nope. She got her a new man.

MARLA: I think he's a junior. And he drives.[9]

KATORA: Well, if Dory can move on and find somebody else, why are you mad that her ex is doing the same thing?

(*Janey, Juanita, and Marla are silent for a moment as they think about this. Suddenly Taylor reenters and makes the announcement with jubilation.*)

TAYLOR: She ran out!

JUANITA: Out where?

TAYLOR: Out of the whole building! She's gone!

JANEY: Did he follow her?

TAYLOR: Nope. He's still here![10]

(*All except Katora cheer and shout in victory. As Juanita, Marla, and Taylor exit, Janey looks at Katora who has been watching her. They stare at each other for a moment, then Janey opens door and follows her friends.*)[11]

1. Before overtly articulating what Janey thinks of the girl under discussion, we get prejudicial details: tight, skimpy dress, the suspicion of dyed hair.

2. This establishes that Katora is a visitor, an outsider. This gives you

license to use low-context exposition. As an outsider, Katora wouldn't know the details of the personal lives of the girls at this school, so Janey and the others have cause to fill her in.

3. "Everybody" implies that they view the girl in question as being trampy.

4. The audience is beginning to connect their animosity toward the girl in question with Dory. Given the ages and behavior of the girls in this scene, the audience is likely to infer that there is a triangle involved, that Dory is their friend, and that the girl they're dissing is viewed as an interloper.

5. The tightness of the clique and their shared focus is reinforced by the fact that Taylor automatically knows the topic of conversation.

6. Occupying the toilets so that Veronica can't use one is a very strong negotiation over space.

7. Good reinforcing use of negotiation over sound.

8. Continued strong use of space, both in the way the girls block Veronica and how Katora distances herself from their action.

9. That Dory's new boyfriend would be considered an improvement because he's a junior (and so presumably older than the previous boyfriend) and that he drives (again in contrast to the earlier boyfriend) underscores our likely view of these girls' values are pretty pathetic. Also, that Dory has so quickly found a new boyfriend suggests that her mating habits are not so different from those of the hated Veronica.

10. That Veronica's date (and Dory's old boyfriend) didn't follow Veronica when she ran from the dance in a distressed state tells us a fair amount about him as well.

11. The final beats suggest that it's more important for Janey to maintain her status with her friends than it is to fulfill her responsibility as Katora's host, even though Katora is family.

All told, this is a very successful piece. Veronica is established as an offstage character through the girls' dialogue, and, when she enters, her status as an outsider is underscored by the humiliation the girls visit upon her. Dory never makes an appearance, but she is also characterized, both by who she chooses as friends and by her reported behavior. And, as I mentioned, Dory's ex-boyfriend is also characterized by his lack of consideration for Veronica.

Many of the other techniques I've discussed are effectively used in this scene—negotiations over objects and space, high- and low-context exposition, violation of convention, and so on. In only a handful of pages, one gets a very vivid picture of this cliquish world and the dismaying values of these young girls. Though Katora doesn't moralize, her contrasting behavior and the questions she asks help establish her as being on a different moral plane than the others. That the girls—including her cousin—abandon her after she implies her disapproval shows the process of ostracization continuing.

CLOSING THOUGHTS

VIOLA SPOLIN TOLD ME SHE CAME UP WITH HER THEATRE GAMES AS she recognized the need for them. In the 1930s, she worked with a troupe of young actors in a WPA project in Chicago. As she saw them encounter problems in the shows she was mounting, rather than bark out orders detailing how to say a line or what gesture to make, she preferred to invent games, the playing of which would help the performers find good choices themselves. As I understand it, she continued to invent, develop, and modify her games up to the last workshop she ran.

I have tried to adapt her approach in the way I work with writers. As I recognize recurring problems in their work (and, for that matter, in mine), my impulse is to try to figure out tactics to address them. This book is intended to share these tactics.

As I've mentioned before, these tactics can be applied in combinations. For instance, one might reinforce a roles-in-conflict scene through the way a character's differing roles use an object. A character who is allowing a personal principle overwhelm a professional imperative may express this by violating the normal rules of the space in which the scene is set.

I don't claim that if you've successfully worked your way through these assignments you're ready to make a place on your wall for a Master of Dramatic Technique certificate. But my hope is that you will find that some of the writing problems you previously approached by relying on instinct and "feel" can now be engaged more consciously.

In a section titled "Useful Publications" in one of the editions of the

Theatre Communications Group's otherwise useful *Dramatists Sourcebook*, the editors tossed out this little nugget: "We have purposely left out any 'how to' books on the art of playwriting because we do not want to promote the concept of 'writing-by-recipe.'" The idea that any work that explores issues of technique may be dismissed as a "how to" or "writing-by-recipe" book strikes me as reductive and petulant.

But there are those who persist in holding a romantic vision of playwriting as something beyond the reach of rational synthesis. I think this in turn reinforces a common view of the writer as child, a person through whom a muse speaks—less a conscious, intelligent creator than the channel the muse has chosen as an instrument to deliver the work.

As a result, there are a lot of directors and producers who believe that a play needs to be protected from the writer who created it. Happily, I am in the position of having have a fair amount of say about who directs major productions of my work, but writers facing their first stagings may well have directors assigned to them. Writers do themselves and their work no favor if they approach rehearsals without being able to articulate to their collaborators in concrete terms what this passage or that bit of business is intended to accomplish. The more you know, the better the basis for your claim to be a grown-up meriting the respect due to a professional.